FOOTBALL SCOUTING METHODS

STEVE BELICHICK
U. S. NAVAL ACADEMY

Martino Publishing
Mansfield Centre, CT
2010

Martino Publishing
P.O. Box 373,
Mansfield Centre, CT 06250 USA

www.martinopublishing.com

ISBN 1-57898-923-X

© *2010 Martino Publishing*

Cover design by T. Matarazzo

Printed in the United States of America On 100% Acid-Free Paper

FOOTBALL SCOUTING METHODS

STEVE BELICHICK

U. S. NAVAL ACADEMY

THE RONALD PRESS COMPANY • NEW YORK

Library of Congress Catalog Card Number: 62–16772

PRINTED IN THE UNITED STATES OF AMERICA

Foreword

In 1957, the Navy football team came up to the annual game with Army with a special problem: How to defense an Army team that was leading the Nation in scoring and rushing offense, with its backfield powered by the twin all-Americans, Pete Dawkins and Bob Anderson.

Navy won the game, 14 to 0, with hardly a serious threat to its goal line. How, then, did the Midshipmen bring it off? Eddie Erdelatz, Navy's head coach, pointed to a broad-beamed assistant who looked like a former pro league fullback, and said simply "He won today's game for us two weeks ago."

"He" was Steve Belichick, who had brought to Erdelatz his final scouting report on Army. It was a voluminous evaluation of Army's skills and tactics. More important, Belichick had detailed how they could be countered by jiggering Navy's defenses. But in the briefing room, Belichick did not content himself with defenses. For Erdelatz he also charted the Navy offense best calculated to exploit every Army soft spot.

Erdelatz had another name for Belichick. "My Upstairs Coach," he called him. It is from the scouting coops high above the stadium that Belichick works, with his charts, his field glasses, his bundle of pencils and his pipe. He has been one of football's best-known figures for more than a decade, traversing the continent in espionage against Navy's future opponents.

If Belichick looks, in size and in slightly-battered countenance, like a former pro fullback, he was, with the Detroit Lions. That was after he came out of Western Reserve in 1941. He knows football as a head coach, too, at Southwestern Louisiana in the Navy's V-12 program and at Hiram Ohio College.

Vanderbilt sought his talents as backfield coach in 1949, and in 1953 North Carolina grabbed him off as chief scout. This is the man that Erdelatz, the perfectionist, coveted for Navy and quickly promoted to Number One scout.

At Navy, Belichick is as much of a fixture as Dahlgren Hall. When Erdelatz retired in favor of Coach Wayne Hardin, Belichick agreed to stay on. Three straight Navy victories over Army have followed.

In all of the football scouting fraternity, no man is more competent to author the handbook of the profession than Steve Belichick. It is a privilege to author this foreword. The dissemination of Steve Belichick's kind of scouting cannot but be an adornment to the game of football.

Shirley Povich
Washington Post and Times-Herald

Preface

Scouting has been one phase of football generally neglected by authors and lecturers. Many outstanding coaches have written about the different systems of offensive football, the various defensive phases of the game, as well as the methods of developing skills in individual players. Usually, however, only an occasional chapter of a book or a few minutes out of an entire lecture is devoted to football scouting, and even then normally deals only with how to *use* scouting information. Thus, a young coach, or any coach with a limited background in scouting, has been deprived of information from authoritative sources about the techniques and knowledge of *how* to scout. In order to obtain information about an opponent, it is imperative that a scout know how to observe each aspect of the game so that he can present a satisfactory and useful report.

This book sets forth some of the methods which can be used to scout the different phases of football, with particular emphasis on the specific things to look for while scouting an actual game, as well as on the analysis of scouting material. It is the hope of the author that this book not only will prove helpful to the novice scout, but also will encourage the development of new ideas and methods in football scouting by experienced and novice scout alike. Scouting can, and should, present an absorbing challenge to the coach, and not the least of his rewards is his pride and satisfaction in a job well done.

The author is particularly indebted to William M. Edwards for his assistance and guidance in this most fascinating phase of football; to Shirley Povich, the gifted columnist of the *Washington Post,* for preparing the foreword to this book; to Captain John I. Hopkins, U.S.M.C., for preparing the drawings; and to the fine coaching associates at Vanderbilt University, the University of North Carolina, and the United States Naval Academy who contributed greatly in the development of many of the methods described in these pages.

Steve Belichick

United States Naval Academy
Annapolis, Maryland
April, 1962

Contents

1

A Case for Specialization
in Scouting

For many years football scouting has been an accepted and important phase of the game. The objective of scouting has been, and still is, to get as much useful information about a future opponent as possible. A more practical objective, however, seems to be to get as much usable information as can be utilized to either (1) help formulate game plans, or (2) better prepare various individual players to either combat the strength, or take advantage of the weaknesses of an individual or an opposing team. It appears that if any information obtained does not fall into one of those two categories, then it is worthless.

Football has undergone many changes in the past few years. It has become a much more complicated game than it was twenty years ago, or even ten years ago. The game is more demanding today than it was several years back, of both the players and the coaches. This is not to be interpreted to mean that players or coaches work harder today than in the past, but to indicate that they have to work on more developed phases of the game. Some thirty years ago the offenses used in football were, for the most part, limited. Defenses were stereotyped, and pass defense took a relatively small amount of practice time, or pregame thought. The coaching staffs were certainly not as large, nor were they as specialized as they are today.

One of the prime reasons for this great advancement in football can certainly be attributed to the wide use and refinement of movies. It was not too many years ago when a football scout could come back with a report on an opponent, and that would be the last and only word on that team. With more teams making use of movies as a coaching aid, however, it was but a matter of time until coaches began to exchange movies with each other. It is believed that the original idea was for one coach to give another coach his movie of a mutual opponent, if that second coach would reciprocate with a film which would be equally beneficial. The coaches in the Southeastern

Conference were among the pioneers in this practice. Many other conferences frowned upon this at first, but now the practice is generally accepted. In many instances it has come to a direct exchange of an agreed number of films between schools.

Undoubtedly one of the prime reasons for getting these movies was to get additional information on opponents to be met, information which could go beyond that obtained by scouting alone. This quite naturally led to the point that coaches knew more about their opponents, and consequently, this led in turn to more and better ways of doing things, both offensively and defensively. If a coach formerly had succeeded in keeping some secrets from the scouts, secrets certainly could not be hidden from the movie cameras.

In this day of modern science and transportation, it is possible for a scout to come back to his school with the movies of the game he saw some twenty-four hours before. Game films can be processed in a matter of hours; the scout can then pick them up and bring them back with him. Most colleges will have received movies of their opponents by Monday, which gives them adequate time to study and utilize information obtained to formulate game plans for a Saturday game. This widespread use of movies has made the scout realize that his work is under close scrutiny, and as a result, his word is no longer necessarily the last word on that opponent.

The question arises in many minds, why scout when movies are available? This seems a logical question, and in fact sometimes the use of movies does cut down on the amount of scouting done. Not all game movies are taken with the same skill, however, or for that matter with the same equipment, and oftentimes the pictures do not show as much as many head coaches would like to see. The wide-scope lens has come into fairly wide use among the major colleges in the nation, but for the smaller schools the equipment used to take this type of picture in many instances is too expensive. Many movies used by colleges today do not, for example, show the defensive backfield men, yet most coaches will agree that a mistake by one backfield man will result in a touchdown or a long gain more often than a mistake made by any other player on the team.

Regardless of whether the accent is on scouting, the use of movies, or a combination of the two methods, it is generally agreed that advance information on an opponent is important and necessary. The ultimate objective is the same. However, the importance of the material increases in proportion to the amount of it that can be absorbed and utilized by the players. If they can not or do not use it, then its value is questionable. The decision of whether it can be carried through to the players is the responsibility of the scout, as well as of the rest of the coaching staff.

Since football has become more complicated, by necessity the scouting reports have also become more complex. The football scout has been able to analyze these more thorough reports, and as a result has come up with many more tendencies and factors to be considered in game preparations than in the past. The point can be reached, and undoubtedly has been, where too much has been given to the players to absorb; they become confused, and in many cases get much less out of a report than they should. Great care should be taken to see that this does not happen. Important strengths and weaknesses must be emphasized, and as much additional material as can be absorbed may be added later.

Basically, every football team has a pattern. It is the purpose of scouting, and the analysis of the scouting, to establish what the pattern is and how to defend as best you can against the strength and take advantage of the weaknesses. Each coach will obviously stress that which he feels his team can do best and will instruct and coach his quarterbacks to call the plays that have been the most successful. Scouting should determine what an opposing team's strength is; then it is up to the staff to determine how to combat this in the most effective ways known. Every effort should be made to stop what the opponent does best. If you are unsuccessful in accomplishing this, it can generally be attributed to two things: first, that adequate preparation was not made, or second, that proper preparation was made, but the opponent had better personnel and you were unable to cope with them. If they had the advantage in personnel, there is little else that could have been done. It is logical to think that a coach's philosophy should be: "Be strong against a team's strength. Be alert for anything that they have shown. If they do beat you, make them do it with something that they haven't shown before."

Although scouting has improved along with the rest of the game of football, it is questionable that it has developed at the same rate or anywhere near the same pace shown for the rest of the game. Scouting has not received the same attention as other phases of the game, at least as far as written material or lectures are concerned. Of the many clinics attended by the author since 1946, never has scouting been a topic of lecture, although every other phase of the game has been discussed from A to Z and back again. There have been many fine books written by talented coaches on many phases of the game, but only an occasional chapter is devoted to scouting. Much more knowledge about this part of football could be disseminated. It would be beneficial to the game as well as to the coaches. This would help to do away with much of the trial and error that the young and inexperienced scout now goes through.

Some factors, however, have been instrumental in the advancement of scouting. The reception of the scouts into the press box, together with the facilities afforded them, has made the scout's work easier and more efficient. It is important to be seated high in the stadium, in a seat perpendicular to the field, and have a place to write in comfort with no need to worry about any uncertainties in the weather. Scouts in the press box are afforded all the courtesies of the press, including prompt delivery of statistics and play-by-play accounts. There are still a number of schools which do not offer these conveniences, but they are diminishing every year. If press box seats are not available, most schools will provide seats for scouts to sit together in an area where the field of vision is excellent. A scout usually receives the utmost courtesy from the school he visits.

Although many phases of football and scouting have changed and improved, there is still a wide-spread belief among many coaches that scouting is not a special skill and that practically everybody on the staff should scout during the year. From the moment a young coach enters the profession, he knows that as soon as the season begins he is undoubtedly going to be asked to scout. Those beginners who have an opportunity to get some background by accompanying an experienced coach on a scouting assignment are indeed fortunate. Many are sent out with little more training than that which they received when they played the game. This becomes very evident when one sits close to many such inexperienced coaches in press boxes throughout the country.

One instance during the 1959 season readily stands out. The scout had a truly outstanding career as both a college and professional player, but this was undoubtedly one of his first ventures as a scout. He was utterly bewildered as the defensive team jumped from one defense to another. It was a relatively simple maneuver, since all the team did was go from a Wide 6 defense to a Split 6 defense, or reverse the procedure. He was so upset in his own mind because he could not analyze the defenses that he was able to get little the team did on offense, since he could not concentrate on it.

A similar incident took place during the 1960 season, when two young and obviously inexperienced coaches were scouting a traditional foe to be met in two weeks. The opponent of the team they were scouting was running from both an unbalanced and balanced line, but they were not aware of it. They had great difficulty in determining what defenses their future opponent was using because of the varying offensive picture. One time the middle guard would be over the offensive center, and possibly the next time he would be over one of the guards to the unbalanced side of the line. This went undetected until the fourth quarter when finally it was called to their attention by another scout. Once they were aware of this varying offensive picture, they were able to salvage something from their afternoon at the game. However, they certainly did not get all the information about that team that they should have been able to get. Needless to say, both games were lost by the teams whose scouts were confused. It is possible that such confusion could have been the contributing factor, because neither head coach of the schools involved could have had the information about his opponent that he should have had in order for his players to go into the game as well prepared as they might have. The scouts should not be blamed entirely, as they surely wanted to do as well as they could on the basis of their knowledge, preparation, and experience. Somebody on the staff should have made an effort to give them some background on scouting—and it is questionable whether they should have been assigned such important games.

It does seem strange that some head coaches feel that any coach, regardless of experience, can scout a football game. This is not necessarily true. It takes a coach with at least an interest in scouting, plus a varied knowledge of different phases of the game, to become a good scout. An interest in scouting is of prime importance, and acceptance of the challenge that it offers will overcome, to some extent, inexperience. Quite naturally, no one can start out with experience, so what does the inexperienced coach do to gain knowledge and background that will be beneficial? Several things that can be done will be dealt with in the next chapter.

SETTING UP A SCOUTING SCHEDULE

There are many different ways scouting schedules can be set up within a coaching staff, whether it be high school or college. These can be dictated by size of the staff, by finances, by conference rules, and by the wishes of the head coach. Regardless of what governs the scouting setup at any school, the author feels a mistake is made unless the same coaches on the staff do all of the scouting. More can be said in favor of this system than can be said against it.

One of the most common arrangements in use today is to have one scout follow a team for a set number of games and then use him in the press box on the day of the game with that opponent. He may be upstairs with a coach or coaches who have the press-box responsibility every week, or he may be up there alone. If a coach follows a team for three weeks, he should have that team well scouted and be very familiar with everything the team does. On the day of the game it should be a simple matter for him to spot any innovations from what he has seen that opponent do in the past. Any changes noted can be called to the attention of the head coach, who can decide what adjustments can be made.

If a staff is large enough, there may be two scouts assigned to scout a team for a fixed number of games. When there are two scouts working together, there must be an understanding of how they are going to divide the work. One effective way is for one to do all the writing when the team is on offense, while the other is the observer. When the team is on defense, this procedure is then reversed. How the responsibility is divided will usually depend upon the scout's coaching responsibility and his knowledge. Some defensive coaches like to observe the offense so they can see how the team is playing in order to start thinking and planning then and there on how best to stop it. Other defensive coaches prefer to observe the defense and analyze the defenses used as the game progresses, to determine the team's strength and weakness. Another method is to have one coach do all the writing for a quarter, with the second coach doing the observing. This procedure is then reversed at the end of that period. Individual coaches will have to decide which method is to be employed. The determining factor should be which one is felt to be the most effective as far as those coaches are concerned.

There are occasions when one man may scout a team throughout the entire schedule. This was used at Navy in 1959 and 1960, and has proven to be very successful. Captain J. P. Monahan, U.S.M.C., saw Army play every game those two seasons and "had the book on them," so to speak. In the eighth and ninth games that Army played, other scouts were assigned to work with him. Each had specific assignments to carry out, such as watching certain individuals, both offensively and defensively. The scouts were used to check on various things on which Captain Monahan wanted more information.

Another method is the one used at the Naval Academy against all opponents except Army. One scout is assigned to follow an opponent for at least two weeks, if the schedule permits. All the information from those games is compiled and presented to the head scout for study and background information. The head scout then observes that team the week prior to its game with Navy. This has the advantage of the same scout's presenting the head coach, the staff, and the squad with the same basic type of report for every opponent. One reason for its use at the Naval Academy is the great turnover of scouting personnel, since many of the coaches used in scouting are military personnel assigned to duty there. At the completion of their duty, they are replaced by other officers who will be used as scouts along with their primary duties. This is a method which can be used by any staff that may include some inexperienced scouts.

A variation of this method is to have two, or possibly three, scouts assigned to watch only the game played the week prior to their game with that opponent. No other game played by that team is personally scouted by a member of the staff, providing the game to be scouted is against a major opponent using an offense from which a true defensive picture can be obtained. If that week the opponent is playing a "breather" or a team whose offense is very different, then some other game on the schedule is chosen to be scouted by members of the staff. When this method is used, however, prior arrangements should be made to obtain films of the games not scouted, either by direct exchange, or from the previous opponents. These films should be available early in the week of the game for study by the other members of the staff. The information obtained from these films is then added to that gained from the game scouted. If and when movies are obtained of the game scouted, they can be closely scrutinized to see if anything went unobserved or unnoted by the scouts.

Often conferences will have restrictions as to the number of times a team may be scouted. Some will limit a team to three "looks," which means one man can see a team three times, or one man can see them once and the following week two men can scout them, or three men can see them in one game. There are some conferences that limit a team to two "looks," while other conferences restrict the scouting to one game, but two scouts may be present. However, usually when there are restrictions as to the number of times that a team may be observed, provisions are made for a film exchange between the two teams. The number of films that can be exchanged might also be limited. This method has the advantage of giving a school with fewer coaches and less resources the same coverage as that of other schools which may be in a better position financially.

These restrictions are sometimes hard to monitor, and there have been cases in which these rules have been slightly infringed upon. One instance that comes to mind took place in a conference which previously had, but no longer has, a scouting restriction as to the number of games that could be seen. One coach had as many as eleven former players attend all the home games of an important opponent. All these players lived close enough to the school, so little expense was involved in getting them to the game. They would meet before the game and divide the responsibility so that each person would have something definite to watch. This generally coincided with something they were familiar with from their playing days. They would each have a small pad on which they would number the plays, both offensively and defensively, and note what happened on each play as far as their responsibility was concerned. They would note what their men did on each play offensively, and where he lined up and what he did on each defense. After the game they would put together all their contributions to each play. As a result they had a complete picture of what happened as far as each play was concerned and each defense used. They could also give a fairly clear picture of each player they watched, and therefore had a good report on the personnel. The modern coach might like to have more information than they could offer by that method today, although there are some coaches who would be content to get that much information.

Regardless of what determines the scouting assignments—whether it is the discretion of the head coach, or whether assignments are dictated by conference rules, finances, or the size of the staff, the most efficient system would seem to be one which would include having certain members of the staff specialize in scouting. Every method has some advantages and some disadvantages, but it is logical to assume that a coach who scouts every week will become more proficient at scouting than one who does it periodically throughout the season. If some coaches are used exclusively as scouts, then those coaches who are with the team on the day of the game should in turn become more versed in their work. They should better be able to work as a team, whether they be in the press box or on the sideline.

The argument for specialization gets a further boost from the scouts themselves, as most scouts agree that they do get more proficient as the season progresses, regardless of whether they scout the same team for several weeks or a different team each week. They can also cite another definite advantage. Friendships and common bonds are developed among the scouts from the different schools. These friendships can lead to an exchange of information and ideas beneficial to all concerned. There are times during a game when a scout may have missed something in a play because of concentration on something at another place on the field. It is not unusual for one scout to ask for information about what he missed of another scout whose friendship has been developed through scouting and whose reliability is established. It is common to hear scouts discuss methods and techniques, as well as the team they are scouting, whenever time permits—before, during, and after a ball game. This is more likely to happen among those scouts who have worked together at games. They have learned to respect the ability and knowledge of each other. This mutual assistance and trust is less likely to develop among strangers or new acquaintances in the scouting field.

Friendships are also cultivated between "regular" scouts and the various head coaches and their staffs of the teams playing the opponents being scouted. The head coach and his assistants can be a valuable source of information for a scout after a game. This important advantage will be discussed further in Chapter 3.

The whole coaching staff benefits from specialization if the same coaching setup is used by the staff every week for every game. Then there is no question that responsibility will be fixed as far as each coach is concerned. If there is any breakdown, it can be pinpointed immediately. When there is a different setup for each game, maximum teamwork can hardly be expected since responsibilities are likely to vary or be confused.

If there are the same two coaches in the press box at every game, each will have definite things to look for. One coach is generally a defensive specialist while the other is an offensive specialist. When the team is on offense, the offensive coach is on the phone and gets assistance from the other coach. When the team goes to defense, this procedure is reversed. With the same coaches on the bench every week receiving the information from the press box, all coaches work more efficiently.

When the same coach or coaches handle the press box phone week after week, they should and will know what they are accountable for, and can make proper preparation to best carry out their assignment. If the scout is not going to be in the press box, then it is up to them to know all they can find out about the opponents. They are going to have to be more familiar with the scouting report and all that it contains. If the opponents make any changes, the press box coaches must detect them and take necessary action.

There can often be a conflict of opinion if the scout is in the press box with the coaches who regularly occupy that vantage point. Since, theoretically, the scout is supposed to know the most about the opponent, what are the limits of his authority to make suggestions? Is he to be used just to detect anything new that is being used by the opponents? Will he have to know the complete offensive and defensive plans of his team for the game? If he has an idea for his team that the coaches who usually occupy the press box reject completely, whose opinion will be transmitted to the coaches on the bench? There are many opportunities for conflict and difference of opinion, and while these are being resolved among the coaches in the press box, often damage is being done on the field and time is wasted.

A coach who knows he is going to scout every week can channel all his effort and extra time to trying to improve himself in this phase of the game. His off-season activity can be devoted to a study of next season's opponents. He can work to improve his techniques as well as the materials he works with. When a coach specializes in scouting, he can make compilation and interpretation of his material easy for his fellow coaches because his forms are standardized and his work of uniform quality. This would be unlikely if all members of a staff scouted, since there are seldom even two coaches who will go to scout a game with the same equipment and the same forms. Specialization has already taken place in most phases of football and could certainly well be carried to that point as far as scouting is concerned.

This system is the one widely used in the professional ranks. Each team has one member of the staff who specializes in scouting, and a regular bench-to-press-box organization prevails. Regardless of the level of football—whether it be high school, college or professional—this is the most efficient organization. On the high school level it would surely pay more dividends than any other method, since the usual high school staff is limited and includes some coaches with little experience. Rather than try to spread themselves out thin and try to become proficient along many lines of football, they could begin by working toward specialization along one definite line as far as game procedure is concerned. It is very demanding of any coach, and especially one in high school, to scout one week, be on the phone upstairs another, and be on the bench a third. Regardless of the size of a staff, as long as there are at least three members including the head coach, a system of assignment can be worked out where uniformity in assignment and stability in organization can be realized. Usually when there is uniformity and stability, there is efficiency, and that can help win football games.

2

Preparations for Scouting

Most football coaches will agree that scouting is an important phase of football and that in order to start formulating game plans, it is essential that correct, concise, and adequate information be submitted by the scout. Most coaches place a great deal of faith and emphasis on scouting reports, and justifiably so. However, it is doubtful that any head coach has gone into a ball game with as much information and background about an opponent as he would desire. By the same token, it is questionable that a scout ever came away from scouting a ball game completely satisfied with his work. There are always a few things that happen in the game which the scout would like very much to have the opportunity to see again. Unfortunately, scouting an actual game does not give him the privilege of rerunning some portion of the game such as he would have in looking at the movies of the game.

Since those who desire all the information possible about an opponent and those who gather the information are seldom completely satisfied, something should be done to try to improve the situation. If the head coach will make an effort to tell the scout specifically what information should be sought in each phase of the game, there will be a marked improvement in the results of the scout's work. The head coach must not expect to get all of the answers in the detail desired, as no scout, regardless of experience, is going to see everything on every play. Once the main objectives are clearly spelled out, the scout should condition himself to concentrate on the most desired items of each phase of the game. Then after obtaining knowledge on these items, he should look for as much other pertinent information as can be observed.

The mere fact that a person knows what is expected of him in scouting a football game does not qualify him to do the job, or infer that he will get the results desired. Regardless of a scout's present football background and knowledge, there was once a first time for him to go on a scouting assignment. How well he did on his first assignment depended upon his coaching background, his knowledge of the various phases of football, and most of all, his preparation for the work to be done. It is a strong and firm belief that to do an adequate job, the scout should have a well-rounded knowledge of the game—more than a mere familiarity with the various phases of the game that he is expected to recognize, appraise, and analyze.

After he is sure of his objectives, one of the first things that the inexperienced scout should do is sit down with the various members of the coaching staff and learn as much as possible about each member's responsibilities in coaching. He must gain as complete a knowledge and understanding of the different aspects of football as is possible. If this is not possible by virtue of the position held, or the background of the assistants, then this background should be sought from other sources such as study of books written by members of the coaching profession, attendance at clinics, and the reading of the professional journals that are available. (This same background should be sought by any coach who has any desire to improve himself in the profession, regardless of whether he is going to scout games or not.) Since most coaches prepare their scouting schedule far in advance of the beginning of the season, there is generally ample time to seek this knowledge and absorb a great deal of it.

Even when a scout has a good background, and has his objectives clearly in mind, he must know how to report his scouting information. Once the form of the final scouting report has been established, the scout should study it endlessly in order to become familiar with all parts of it. If one member of the staff is designated as the chief scout, he should go over the report together with all other scouts so that all phases of it will be clear. A complete understanding must be had of what information is expected from the scout.

Approximately half of the scouting form will be concerned with the team's defense. In order to adequately scout a team's defense, a basic knowledge of defense must be an important part of a scout's preparation. The scout should talk with the defensive coach and get a complete breakdown of the defenses used in football. He should know what each man's responsibility is on each of these defenses. These should be diagramed in detail for future study and reference. (Examples of such diagrams can be found in Chapter 7.) Once the fundamental responsibility of each player on each defense is understood and known, then learn the various stunts used from each defense, and the reasoning behind them, and what a team tries to accomplish by employing such stunts. If a scout does not know the alignment of players and their responsibilities in specific defenses, he can hardly expect to detect a variation of it, or if a defense was attacked successfully at a certain spot, who was responsible for the breakdown.

There are many adjustments that can be made in defenses employed in football in order to compensate for the different flankers that are used by the offenses. These should also be fully understood, and the reasoning behind them known. These adjustments often concern the linemen as well as the backs, and to know what these can be is to help recognize them when they are seen in a game. It is not enough for the scout to be familiar with only the defenses and the adjustments that his team uses, but he must have a knowledge of all defenses and their variations.

It would be most unusual for the head coach not to desire also as much information as possible about the pass defense of the opponents. In order for the scout to do an adequate job in this field, it is most beneficial to have a working knowledge of the various types of pass defense employed in football today. Fundamentally, pass defense breaks down into the categories of zone defense, man-to-man defense, and a combination of man-to-man and zone defense. A vast majority of teams in college and high school football use a zone defense, but it is important to know exactly what type of pass defense a team utilizes. Some teams will have two different types of pass defense, while others will use different types of zone coverage. Using two types of pass defense is the exception rather than the rule.

The defensive alignment of the backs is either a three deep, or a two or four deep, depending on the terminology used by the coach. Teams can and do use the different types of pass defense from each of these backfield alignments. In order for a scout to be able to do a creditable job of scouting pass defense, he should have a knowledge of that phase of the game which will enable him to recognize the type used. Once the type is established, then he can think in terms of finding weaknesses in either the defense or the personnel.

To go one step further in learning about defense, the coach should know how the passing and running responsibilities of the various players are tied together. It is important to understand how the backfield men are tied into the running defense as well as how the linebackers and some of the linemen can be part of the pass defense. For example, it is not uncommon to see the middle guard, and one or both ends, drop off into pass defense from the Oklahoma 5–4 defense on certain long-yardage situations.

Since there are many football teams which use the unbalanced line all or some of the time during a ball game, the scout should become familiar with the defensive adjustments that are made to meet this type of offense. Some defenses will look entirely different when seen against an unbalanced line. At times the middle guard on an odd defense will be head-on the center, while at other times he will be head-on the guard to the heavy side of the line. Often where the middle guard lines up will determine the alignment of the defensive backfield. Since the position of the middle guard on an odd defense can be varied, many different pictures can result, and the scout should be familiar with all of them. It is a good idea to take all the defenses that you are learning and set them up against both a balanced and un-balanced line, and learn them accordingly.

With a fundamental knowledge of all aspects of defense at his command, the inexperienced scout can be expected to do a more efficient job in covering this phase of the game.

This preparation to scouting should now be carried to the offensive phase of football, both running and passing. The line blocking of the running offense should be understood as well as backfield maneuvers, and also backfield blocking. Probably the simplest approach in learning about the running offense is to become familiar with as many different type blockings as possible for each offensive hole. That is, know the many different and most effective ways to block for a sweep, off-tackle, as well as the inside plays, using both trap and straight blocking. These should be known against the various defenses, since generally there is some difference when the defenses are altered. These methods of blocking should be catalogued for future study and reference, and if in your scouting or study of the game, you should learn of some method that you are unfamiliar with, diagram it and add it to your file. It is amazing how many times you will likely have occasion to refer to it in the future.

Know and understand the use of flankers since many T-formation teams make wide use of them. What part does the use of flankers and split ends play in a team's offense? If you know what may be done with these different offensive alignments, you are better able to tell whether a team utilizes them in its offense, or simply employs them as "window dressing."

Although the single wing offense is not in such wide use as the T formation at the present, it would be advantageous to know as much about this offense as you can. Many T-formation teams utilize some features of the single wing to a large degree. There are several excellent books available on this phase of football. The reading and study of these books should be very profitable.

The unbalanced line is becoming more popular in present-day football and a study should be made of this phase of the game. The experienced scout will see many things in an offense using the unbalanced line that are different from those in an offense run by a team employing a balanced line. For example, there is a difference in blocking on many plays, since the unbalanced-line offense will utilize a tackle that pulls and leads the play, a maneuver not used with any regularity from a balanced line.

A good basic knowledge of pass offense is important to the scout. There are not many teams in the nation that stress the passing game to the extent that they do the running game, so some outside study on this phase could be very helpful. Here, too, there are many good books available which will cover all aspects of patterns, pass protection, as well as the individual skills which are necessary to an effective passing attack. The scout should know the theories as well as principles used to attack the various types of pass defense that are in use. If a scout is going to be asked for recommendations of offensive plays to use against an opponent, it is imperative that he have some knowledge of running and pass offense.

This search for knowledge should also include discussion with a coach who has background in the kicking game. There are various types of punt formations, and each has some advantages and disadvantages that should be known to the scout. An understanding of the different punt rushes and returns as well as some of the kickoff returns that teams employ would be beneficial to a scout.

There are different philosophies of football. These should be explored thoroughly to see what the different viewpoints are, and who are their exponents. There are coaches who feel that ball control strategy is the best, if backed up with a strong running game. The forward pass is of little consequence in their thinking. There are a few coaches in college ranks who possibly go overboard on the passing game to the extent that their running attack is a poor threat. Then there are some who say that they believe in a balance between the two methods, but team statistics do not substantiate the claim of a large percentage of these coaches—it is usually found that the running offense completely dominated the statistics.

Coaches will also differ on game strategy. Some coaches tell their quarterbacks to run a play that has been successful until it is stopped. Other coaches will instruct them to save that play until the yardage is needed to keep a drive going. Some signal callers are restricted to certain plays by the position on the field. For them, the football field is divided into different zones. Their nearness to the goal line zone, for example, determines on what down they should punt, whether they can throw a pass or not, and the type of play that they are permitted to run. Other coaches will give their quarterbacks the freedom to run any play they want, providing they have a good reason for calling that particular play. There are many different viewpoints as to game strategy, and it would be well to become familiar with as many of them as possible. A good scout should be able to determine the coach's strategy after he has scouted the team a few times.

In order to build up this background of knowledge on the different phases of the game of football, it is necessary that considerable time be spent studying it. This knowledge cannot be obtained in a matter of several days, or even several weeks. The desire to learn should not wane, since every year there are new wrinkles added to every phase of the game. When anything new comes to your attention, try to find out the particulars of it. The chances are excellent that somewhere along the line in your future scouting, you are going to run into it.

As a scout seeks knowledge to broaden his background in football through study and conversation with other coaches, he should also make every effort to study movies in order to develop techniques which will be beneficial in scouting. Movies can be an excellent aid in developing ability to recognize formations, various flankers and plays, as well as defensive alignments. You should see how quickly you can recognize these various things as they appear on the screen. You should also learn to increase your ability to detect how offensive plays develop in different ways, as described in Chapter 8. This can be accomplished by work and concentration.

Every scout, and especially one new to the assignment, should spend considerable time "breaking down" movies in their entirety. This means looking at a movie of a football game and charting the alignment, assignment, and execution of every move of every player visible on the screen. By doing this, the scout will find that nothing will escape his eye, and that much more can be learned about a team this way than by simply looking at the movie and recording the obvious information. Unless the movie is "broken down," what some teams or players are really doing often does not become completely apparent. This is the way that you uncover tip-offs, and these will inspire you to look for more. This should definitely be done with movies of an opponent that is to be scouted, and should include more than one movie. In order to simulate a scouting assignment, the information obtained should be analyzed and put into a final scouting form like the one which will be submitted during the season.

After the report is completed, the scout should study all phases of his report and formulate his impressions of that team from the habits and tendencies that are shown by his report. He should learn the team's method of blocking, its favorite pass patterns, the features of its kicking game, as well as the defenses employed—and all aspects of those defenses. When this information is learned, another movie of that team should be obtained. Then as you look at the second movie, try to anticipate what the opponents will do before they actually do it. With this background and practice, it will be considerably easier to scout that team when you see it play. It will be found that most of what it does will be very similar to what was seen in the movies.

Quite generally it is found that football teams will vary very little in their over-all pattern from one season to the next. There may be a difference in one phase of the game, but seldom more than that. Even if there is a difference, it is unusual to find a real change in the coach's philosophy of the game. Between seasons a head coach is not likely to change from a firm believer in a strong running attack to a proponent of a passing attack, except on very rare occasions. An exception that stands out is Colonel Earl Blaik, who was a leading disciple of a vicious running attack, which was the basis of his offensive thinking. However, prior to the 1958 football season, he changed his offensive alignment, retained a strong running game, but utilized the forward pass much more than he had in previous years. It appeared that his basic philosophy of the game remained the same as far as his ground game was concerned, but he did alter his thinking about passing. In scouting Army prior to 1958, I personally felt that anytime Army threw a pass, generally Army was doing offensively the thing the team did second best. Since Army had such a strong running game, play passes were used with effectiveness, but the total passing attack was not as dangerous as the running. However, during the 1958 season, one phase of the offensive attack was just as explosive as the other, and the utmost respect had to be shown to both phases, with possibly a little more to the passing. This change in a team's offense from one season to the next is more generally the exception than the rule.

When studying movies to develop techniques to be employed in scouting a football game, it must be remembered that you will not get the same view as you will when actually scouting a football game. The pictures are generally taken from a higher elevation than you will be able to get. Movies often have the benefit of telescopic lenses that bring the action closer to you than it would actually be in a game, and consequently you get a closer and more detailed look than you do from scouting the game from the stands or the press box. On a screen the action is confined to a much smaller area than a football field, which gives a different perspective. Still, effective habits can be created and developed by studying movies, if a definite effort is made to condition oneself to look for certain things.

Today, with the great advancements in and availability of photographic equipment, much can be learned from the use of slides. Pictures can be made of any number of offensive and defensive alignments and then made into slides for study. These can be flashed on a screen for a limited period of time so the scout can test himself and see if he can distinguish what was shown. The habit can be developed to learn to look at the total picture, and thus a scout is able to distinguish the most predominant formations and defenses used in football. This method can also be used to develop the technique in learning to distinguish defenses, described in Chapter 5. The steps of progression can be taken by the scout and made into slides. Then he can develop his ability to recognize different defenses by controlling the length of time that the picture appears on the screen.

If a scout has made the preparation described to improve his knowledge of the game, and in addition views movies of the teams that he is going to scout, he will find that he will be able to do a more complete and efficient job. Again it must be emphasized that if a scout knows as much about the game as is possible, and is familiar with all phases of the game, it will be apparent that he will be able to recognize the things he must look for much quicker and more easily.

Since a scout will have the opportunity to see many football teams in action, both on the field as well as via movies, he should keep organized and descriptive diagrams of all phases of the game that will benefit him. The various defenses should be kept in one notebook and the offenses in another.

These should be well indexed so that when one comes up for discussion, it will be a simple matter to find it and refer to it.

The offensive running plays should be indexed according to the offensive hole through which they are run. Passes can be indexed by formation. They can be further classified as roll-out, drop-back, screen, or play-action passes.

There are various methods used to index defenses. It is possible to organize some defenses by the formation they are used against—such as single wing, split-T, winged-T, "Lonesome End," and spread formations. Other defenses will be indexed according to whether they are odd or even defenses, that is, depending on whether there is a man head on the offensive center (odd defense), assuming a balanced line. As many different blocking assignments as can be found to use against the many defenses employed in football should be kept on record. If, on some occasion, you are to meet a defense that your team has not played against for some time, you can refer to your notebooks and possibly incorporate some different blocking in your plans.

This happened in a recent football season when Navy was to meet a team that used the Eagle 5–4 defense, one which had not been used against Navy to any extent in the recent past. Ernie Jorge, the offensive line coach, checked through his notes and found several types of blocking which he had seen used with great success against this type of defense. They are shown in Figs. 2–1 and 2–2, and proved to be very effective. This special blocking was incorporated into the offense to be used against this defense. These plays were so successful that the opposing team was forced out of the Eagle 5–4 defense early in the ball game. This is one example of the usefulness of a notebook. It is doubtful that these plays and the special blocking would have been committed to memory.

In Fig. 2–1, the right end releases to the outside of the linebacker and goes downfield to block the left safety man. The right tackle pulls and traps the middle guard as the right guard blocks the defensive left tackle out. The center steps toward the middle guard to set him up for the right tackle, as well as to permit the left guard to go through and seal beyond the hole. After using an influence block on the middle guard, the center then blocks the tackle to his left. The left tackle turns out on the right linebacker as the left end releases to the outside to get the right safety man. The fullback starts out by aiming for the outside leg of the right guard to help "freeze" the defensive tackle and linebacker, and then veers to the inside. The quarterback uses an open pivot to hand off to the fullback and continues on with his fake to the left halfback, who runs off tackle.

In Fig. 2–2, the same backfield action is employed to make the plays look identical. The right end steps toward the linebacker to set him up for the trapping guard, and then the end turns out and blocks the defensive end.

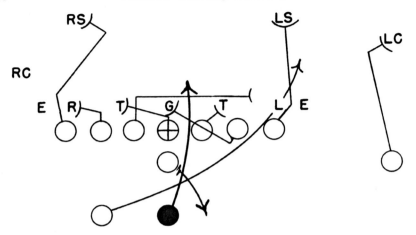

Fig. 2–1. A special type blocking against the Eagle 5–4 defense.

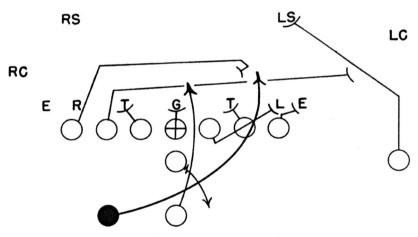

Fig. 2–2. A companion play for Fig. 2–1.

The right tackle blocks the defensive tackle in, while the center blocks the middle guard. The left guard blocks out on the right defensive tackle, and the left tackle and end release across field to block the defensive secondary. This same blocking can be used effectively against the Wide 6 defense, providing the play is run from the normal T formation, and the right halfback goes behind the right guard and blocks the linebacker, as shown in Fig. 2–3.

Another example of effective and unusual blocking which was kept on

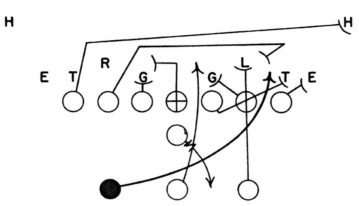

Fig. 2–3. A special type blocking against the Wide 6 defense.

file for future reference is shown in Fig. 2–4. This blocking has been used successfully by some teams against the Oklahoma 5–4 defense. This is designed to work against linebackers who key the offensive guards, and it helps to set up excellent trap blocking on the tackle. However, to be effective, it must be used with three backs in.

The right end releases for downfield blocking. The right tackle sets up as he would on pass protection and then blocks the end. The right guard

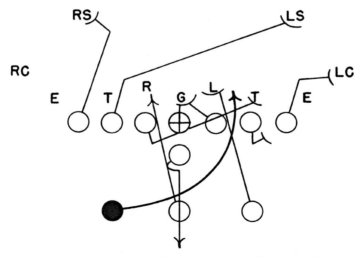

Fig. 2–4. A special type blocking against the Oklahoma 5–4 defense.

and center double team the middle guard, while the left guard traps the defensive left tackle. The left tackle and left end go down field to block the defensive safeties. The right halfback "cheats up" a little and blocks the left linebacker as he prepares to play the trap. The fullback fills where the guard pulled, and the left halfback carries the ball on an inside cross-buck.

Unless blocking like this is copied and filed away in a notebook or other suitable place, it is often forgotten, and when the need for it arises, memory will not be as reliable as you would like it to be. The same holds true of defenses that might be seen or heard discussed.

One of the most helpful phases of schooling that can benefit an inexperienced scout is to work at a game with a scout who has had considerable experience. Here he can observe the seasoned scout in action, noting how he goes about his work, what he looks for, what he records, etc. However, observation alone is good only to a certain point. After that its usefulness is questioned, in that the novice does not get the benefit of actually doing the work and receiving the instruction and correction that he needs. At this point it is better to have the experienced scout observe the newcomer in action by having the latter work part of the game. Should anything pertinent be missed by the new scout, the veteran can add it to the play. The beginner can record the down, yardage, position on the field, and hash mark. As the offensive team comes out of the huddle, he can record the formation, then the play itself, along with any relevant information. Should the experienced scout note anything unobserved by the recorder, he can immediately point it out. Such comment might be that the far guard pulled, or the end hooked the opposing end, etc. This makes the beginner more conscious of some of the additional things to look for other than who carried the ball and what hole was attacked. This same type of procedure could be used when the team scouted was on defense.

In using such a method, the beginner has the opportunity to do what he will have to do in the future, but has the benefit of on-the-job training. The teacher is present for the express purpose of scouting the game, and can do his job and at the same time give advice and instruction to the novice. If this schooling can take place over a period of several games, the work can eventually be divided so that the recording and observing can be alternated by quarters—or can be divided in any other way desired. When this method is used, the beginner is told exactly what to look for, in order that he may develop the proper work habits.

At the completion of the game, the report should be prepared by the less experienced scout, but he should be told precisely how everything is to be done so that the uniformity of reports will be maintained.

If the beginner cannot have the benefit of working with an experienced scout, then he must have his plans well set before he goes to the game to scout. He should have a list of what he is going to look for in each phase of the game and must know it thoroughly. With an organized plan and method, good results can be obtained.

3

What Is Expected
of the Scout

There is a misconception among some laymen, and even those in the coaching profession, as to how a football scout does his work and what is expected of him. The laymen seem to believe that much of what a football scout does is carried on in the utmost secrecy. Only scouting that is illegal is done in secrecy. Many football coaches who have done no scouting seem to believe that all scouts work in the same manner and seek the same information. Actually, it is unlikely there are any two scouts who work in exactly the same manner, with the same equipment, and seek the same information.

A scout's method of doing his work will be determined by many factors. Some of these factors will include his background, experience in football as well as in scouting, and his knowledge of the game. A scout should never be static in his methods, since the frequent changes in football should cause him to re-evaluate his methods as well as seek ways to improve them from time to time. Whatever the scout's particular method, his objective, as stated before, will remain the same—to secure usable information.

The kind of information that the scout seeks should not be left entirely to his discretion, but should be spelled out in detail by the head coach, or those assistants entrusted with formulating game plans. It is not enough for the head coach to say, "Scout the game and bring back all the information you can." Each head coach should have definite items that he wants to know about. Often, what is of importance to one head coach is of little or no concern to another. It is to be expected that every head coach will want to know the basic offense and defense used, and on a basis of this, what can be anticipated. However, the degree to which the offense and defense is to be analyzed for tendencies varies among the head coaches. Some coaches will want every analysis possible, while others will be content with the basic alignments and adjustments. Each head coach has his own requirements; these are dictated by his philosophy of the game. A coach who advocates and believes in a strong running game will usually be less interested in pass-defense coverage than a coach who favors the passing game. A coach who stresses the kicking game will be much more concerned with how well the safety man handles punts than the coach who believes the only time to give up the football by kicking is on fourth down. Some coaches want to know all the answers about a team that employs the quick kick, while others do not have much interest in that phase of the game. In order for a scout to do a satisfactory job, it is important that he know thoroughly the head coach's philosophy, as well as have a complete understanding with him as to what is expected in the scouting report.

The importance of this understanding was impressed on me while submitting a report to a coaching staff about an opponent which quick kicked. I was told to forget that part of the report, as we would be happy to get the football if that team wanted to quick kick it. It was of no concern how or when it was done. That particular coach felt at that time he did not want to concern his defensive backs with a quick-kick possibility, for fear that they could become so conscious of it they might neglect their other defensive responsibilities. His philosophy was to make no special preparation for that phase of the game, but rather to have the team play football as best they could, and handle the situation when and if it happened in the game. The quick kick was not a part of his attack, nor did it have a place in his thinking as a weapon of football. Undoubtedly there are football coaches who will disagree; these dissenters feel that the quick kick *is* an important weapon of the game. When an opponent utilizes it, the coach wants to know all the details of who does it, how effectively, when it is done, from what formation, and any other points that may be of value. Conversely, the coach who was not interested in the quick kick did, however, want information in the greatest detail about defensive adjustments to flankers. He placed greater emphasis on this than most head coaches because it was important to his philosophy of football.

In order to enlighten the scout as to what will be expected of him, some head coaches, at times with the aid of the rest of the staff, will prepare a check list for the scout to follow. This will enable the scout to have a complete understanding of what is expected of him insofar as his search for information is concerned. Such a check list will cover the different phases of the game about which the scout is expected to bring back information on as many points as possible. Supplementary sheets are provided to diagram the various plays, defenses, and any other pertinent information that can be shown more clearly than explained. These points of value may include punt formations, punt returns or rushes, kickoff returns and aligment, etc. A well-prepared and thought-out check list can provide a head coach with the information needed to formulate game plans.

There are other head coaches who will have a final report form prepared for the scout to use in determining what knowledge he is to seek. This could be a form, or similar to the one, shown in the Appendix. A combination of these two methods can also be used, in which case the scout will have a check list to refer to, as well as a final form to complete. The check list will contain some questions to which the scout will seek the answers, and the final form will ask for specific diagrams, tendencies, etc.

Regardless of what type forms are used, it is important that the scout know where to place the emphasis in his work. Some coaches will want a detailed report on the personnel, while others will stress as complete a picture as possible of the offense and defense, along with the tendencies in each phase of the game. There are still others who want a more complex report, i.e., they will want the offensive and defensive picture, as well as information on the strength and weakness of the players.

After it is decided what is expected of the scout in gathering information and presenting it, it should all be put in writing. The scout can then begin to study and learn what is expected and asked of him. However, this does not necessarily mean that every question will always be answered. The effort should be made to get all information requested, but often this is not possible due to various factors. Weather conditions could be so adverse that a true picture could not be obtained on some phases of the game. The opposition might be such that a team was not compelled to utilize all of its weapons. Certain key players might be temporarily out of the lineup, due to injuries. Such factors may limit a scout's information.

A check-off list given to a scout, pinpointing the different questions that will be asked of him in scouting a game, can be of great value to coaches at all levels. The following sample is one used on the college level, and is one that can be classified as neither complex nor simple. It could be extended or simplified, to comply with the individual wishes of a head coach. The list can also be formulated as a series of questions, with ample room for the answers and diagrams, and could well be a final report. This sample check-off list is preceded by instructions to the scout. These instructions could, of course, be altered to suit any coach's individual beliefs.

SCOUTING CHECK-OFF LIST AND INSTRUCTIONS

GENERAL INSTRUCTIONS

1. Do not permit your interest to be aroused to the point that you become a spectator. This will hinder, and often prevent, you from obtaining essential information. Concentrate on the action that is taking place. It may well be the only time you will see that particular thing happen in the game. In case of doubt about some action, indicate that part of the information as doubtful, or omit it in the report, rather than give erroneous information.

It must be remembered that the primary objective of scouting is to gather as much pertinent information as you can. In order to do this, you must carefully observe and record what the opposition does. It is imperative that *all* action on the field be observed. You should approach your assignment with certain goals fixed in your mind, and with the objective of answering the questions in the check-off list. We want to know what the other team does, not what you think they *could* or *should have done.* We want to know *what they do, how many times they do it,* and *how successful they are.* Do not give them credit for doing or being able to do anything that you have not seen them do.

2. Review any information that can be obtained from previous scouting reports of this or last year, and from movies or newspaper accounts. Should the opponent be new to the schedule, contact some of their previous opponents to see if you can get some information from them. Be willing to trade for any information that they have with any you may gather on that or any other opponent.

3. Before seeing a team for the first time, try to get information about them from scouts who have seen them in action. Try not to go completely cold into the first look at a team. It is important, too, that you get to the game early in order to talk to other scouts. Make an attempt to find out at least the basic offense and defenses that the opponent has been using. It can also be helpful to get comparable information about the team playing against your opponent, as this will make it easier to recognize formations as well as defenses, and any adjustments. During the half-time as well as after the game, in talking to other scouts try to find out about the defenses employed against your opponent in more detail than you have probably been able to observe. Also get the successful running and pass plays used, as well as anything else of value, either well or poorly executed, which could be helpful in formulating your game plans. Be willing to reciprocate with similar information about the team you are scouting.

4. After seeing a team in action once, you should know the numbers of the players who are in the game most of the time. This should include any specialists that see action. Otherwise there is no need to go beyond the first two teams. If there is any deviation from the regular lineups during subsequent games, see if you can analyze the reason.

5. You should always be at the game early enough to get settled and organized to observe the pregame warmup of the opponent. During the warm-up period, observe, appraise and record the passers, punters, centers snapping the ball to the punters, the pass receivers, safety men, as well as the kickoff and field-goal kickers.

6. If you are working with one or more scouts from your staff, plan how you are going to work together, and divide the responsibility of getting the information desired.

7. Complete the report as soon after the game as is possible, when everything is fresh in your mind. After reading some newspaper accounts, review your report, as it is likely that something may be recalled that will be of some value. It is not possible to have recorded at the game all that you have seen. When you have completed your report, analyze it and determine the opposition's weak and strong points in each phase of the game of offense, defense, and the kicking game. Each team will do some things both better and more often than other things. Determining a team's favorite maneuvers will help to establish its pattern, as every team has some type of pattern. After the analysis of the report has been made as to strength, weaknesses, tendencies, and pattern, try to project your analysis to determine the thinking underlying why and when particular things were done. This analysis of the team should be learned by the scout, so if you see the team again, you will know what it has done and will be prepared to see if its overall picture coincides with what has been seen in the past. The full benefit of scouting past games cannot be received unless that information obtained has been thoroughly learned by the scout.

8. Gather the data from all games scouted and condense it into one report for presentation.

9. From all the information obtained, see if you can determine why the team has or has not been successful in the games that you have scouted.

CHECK-OFF LIST FOR THE GAME

Offense

1. While the team is in the huddle, record the down, yardage to go, the yardline and position on the field in relation to the sidelines. At the completion of the play, record the formation, the play and the gain or loss.

2. Get the number of the player in each position. Indicate the number of the substitute that enters the game, as well as the player that is replaced.

3. Know basically what is being used defensively against the team you are scouting.

4. Note the basic line splits as well as any variations that are detected. Check the ends occasionally to see if they vary their split. Be sure to do this on long-yardage or so-called passing situations. Check the stance of the linemen to see if there is any tip-off as to what an individual might do.

5. Note how the team gained possession of the ball to start each offensive series—such as recovered fumble, blocked punt, intercepted pass, held for downs, etc.

6. Determine whether the backs adjust or vary their position to better carry out specific assignments.

7. Observe the flankers and split ends occasionally to see if they serve a definite purpose in the play, or if they are used simply as "window dressing."

8. List the passers. How do you rate them? How deep do they go back to set up to pass? Do they indicate "right now," i.e., as they are setting up to pass, do they show to whom or where they are going to throw the ball?

9. If there are any favorite receivers, be sure to indicate them, and point out their special weapons.

10. Evaluate the pass protection. If the pass protection breaks down, what particular area or player is responsible?

11. Indicate on the play-by-play, any penalties assessed against the team scouted. Note if after a major penalty there are any special type plays run, such as screens, passes, draw plays, or long passes.

12. If they use the two-point play after a touchdown, determine whether it falls into the pattern of short-yardage plays, or if they use something tricky or unusual.

Defense

1. Check and record each defensive alignment, such as Oklahoma 5–4, 6–1, etc., and also record whether the backs are in a two- or three-deep alignment.

2. Know what defensive adjustments are made from each defense to each type flanker and split end used against them.

3. On an odd defense, note how far off the ball the middle guard and two tackles play. On an even defense, check the depth of the guards and tackles. If they are lined up approximately a foot or more off the ball, be alert for slanting, looping, or stunting by these players. If they vary their position or depth, try to determine the reason for it. Note any "stacking" (one defensive player lining up directly in back of another) of any defensive players. This usually indicates stunting by the players involved.

4. Check to see if any of the defensive men have a big stagger in the alignment of their feet. If the team does any slanting, looping, or stunting, be sure to check the feet of the defensive linemen and linebackers to see if there is any tip-off as to the direction they are going.

5. Determine what linemen and what side of the line is the strongest.

6. Observe the depth and position of the linebackers to see if they vary their alignment. If they do, try to determine the reason. Again, this could be an indication of stunting defenses, or that the linebackers are getting into a more advantageous position to take care of their responsibility. Some linebackers have a tendency to deepen on a passing situation and get closer to the line when they are going to "shoot." Notice how active the linebackers are. How effective are they on plays run at them as well as on plays run away from them? Do they get to their pass-defense responsibility quickly? What angle do they take in going back?

7. Designate which linebacker is the best against running plays, and which is best on pass defense.

8. Determine which, if any, of the linemen get into the pass defense. If they do, who are they, and how effective are they?

9. See how well the line rushes the passer. Who seems to do the best job at this? Is the team vulnerable to screen passes or draw plays?

10. Observe the depth and action of the defensive backs on running plays. On plays to their side, do they come up fast? Could any of them be fooled by a play-action pass? On plays away from them, do they take the proper pursuit course? Try to determine on whom the defensive backs are keying.

11. Establish what type pass defense the team employs. Who are the best and who are the weakest defenders? Were the opponents of the team scouted particularly successful in passing against any individual, or in any one area or zone?

12. Record whether, if the team was leading late in the first half or late in the game, a "Prevent" defense was used. (This is a defense where the backs, linebackers and possibly the ends get deep to prevent the completion of a long pass.)

13. When the opponent uses a short-yardage or goal-line defense, designate which, if any, backs get into or up on the defensive line. Where do they line up?

Kicking Game: Punts, Rushes and Returns

1. Observe the type of punt formation used, indicate the splits employed and the depth of the kicker. How well does the center snap the ball back to the kicker under pressure?

2. Know how well the punter kicks with, and also without, rushing. What type of kicks are they—as to height and distance?

3. Ascertain whether the kicking game is employed as part of the game strategy, or if it is used only to give up the ball as a result of field position.

4. Record how well kicks are covered. Is any one exceptionally good or poor at covering kicks?

5. Watch the opponent's action against punt formation. Is a punt rush used? A punt return? Or are both employed? Which is done most effectively? Are there any tip-offs as to what the opponent is going to do?

6. Indicate whether the quick kick is used. Who quick-kicks, from what formation, and is there any tip-off as to when it might be done?

7. Designate anyone who is dangerous as a punt returner.

Field Goals and PAT's

1. Should the team try a field goal, note who the kicker is, as well as the holder and his depth. How far was the attempt? If it was unsuccessful, was there any indication from pregame observation that the kicker could kick one that far?

2. Record how well field goal attempts are covered.

3. Denote anything other than a kick which is tried from the place-kick formation.

4. Specify who kicks the point after touchdowns.

Kickoff and Returns

1. Note the deployment of the kickoff team and the effectiveness of the coverage. Is the team vulnerable in any specific area to a return? Who is the kicker, and how far can he kick the ball? What player or players are the first ones down under the kick? Who are the safetymen, and how do they play?

2. Record the alignment to receive the kickoff. Are there any especially dangerous receivers, and if so, where are they stationed? What type of returns did the team employ?

POSTGAME SUGGESTIONS

1. The coaches of the team that played against your future opponent can be of great assistance in answering some questions you might have. They may also be able to confirm some impressions that you have formed of the opponent. Try to get into the dressing room to meet and get acquainted with those coaches, if you do not already know them.

2. If that team won, you will, of course, congratulate the coaches on their victory, as well as on their game plans, and the execution of those plans. If possible, try to get their opinions on the opponent. Perhaps one of the coaches will make some statement that will lead you to check on something you might otherwise have overlooked. If you should want to talk with any of the players, make certain that you first have the permission of one of the coaches.

3. If that team lost, do not try to force yourself on the coaches. If and when you do engage them in a conversation, try to find out what they would do differently if they were to play that team again. If any coach is reluctant to talk, never try to pressure him into talking. It might be that at some future time one of the coaches will be more eager to discuss the game, perhaps via telephone.

4. Whether the coaches are interested in giving you information or not, be sure to wish them well in the future. Assure them that you and the other members of your staff will be pleased to assist them in the future in every way possible. It is important to remember that whenever you seek assistance, always be willing to reciprocate, either then or at any future time.

With detailed instructions and a check-off list of this type to be used as a guide, each scout knows what is expected of him. He will want to study his check-off list, as well as the final report form, before each game that is scouted. It is advisable to also review the list during the half-time intermission, in order to recall some phases of the game which may have been overlooked. It is not expected that each point will be covered after seeing a team in action one time. The more times that you see a team play, the more complete your impressions, knowledge and report on that team should be. It is important that each scout get as much of the information requested as possible. Knowing exactly what he must report should make him more efficient as well as more proficient. He realizes that on each phase of the game, he is going to have to obtain the answers to specific questions. As the action takes place on the field, he knows he must condition himself to concentrate on certain items. He will find, however, that it is easier to record something specific, even in great detail, than to try to cover everything generally. A scout will do a much better job if he knows exactly what his objectives are.

4

Worksheet Forms
and Terminology

Long before any scout goes forth on an assignment, he and the other members of his staff should have a complete understanding and agreement as to terminology, descriptive terms, and types of forms to be used in reporting his information. These matters should be resolved long before the season begins, and all printed or mimeographed material should be completed and made ready for use. There are many types of forms that can be used in scouting a football game, but the forms used by one staff, although they can differ in minor respects, should have the same format. This prevents any difficulty and misunderstanding when two or more scouts are working a ball game. The only differences should be in the formations that are predrawn on the forms. Some scouts like to have a complete team shown, as illustrated in Fig. 4–1, while others prefer to have only the five internal linemen, the quarterback, and fullback drawn on the work sheets. Each scout seems to develop a preference for one type, and will work with it week after week. For the beginner, it may be a matter of trial and error for several games, or until it becomes fairly certain which is the easiest for him to work with. This trial and error period should be conducted during the "breaking down" of movies. When a scout works alone all of the time, there is no need for his forms to be exactly the same as those used by the other coaches, so long as he reports complete information in a uniform manner.

OFFENSIVE SCOUTING SHEET

In Fig. 4–1, a partial offensive worksheet of the form used at Navy is shown. There are four formations to a sheet, and all are identical. Forms other than that shown in Fig. 4–1 are made up to comply with the wishes of individual scouts, but these will differ only to the extent of the offensive formation shown. Should a particular scout have a preference for a form

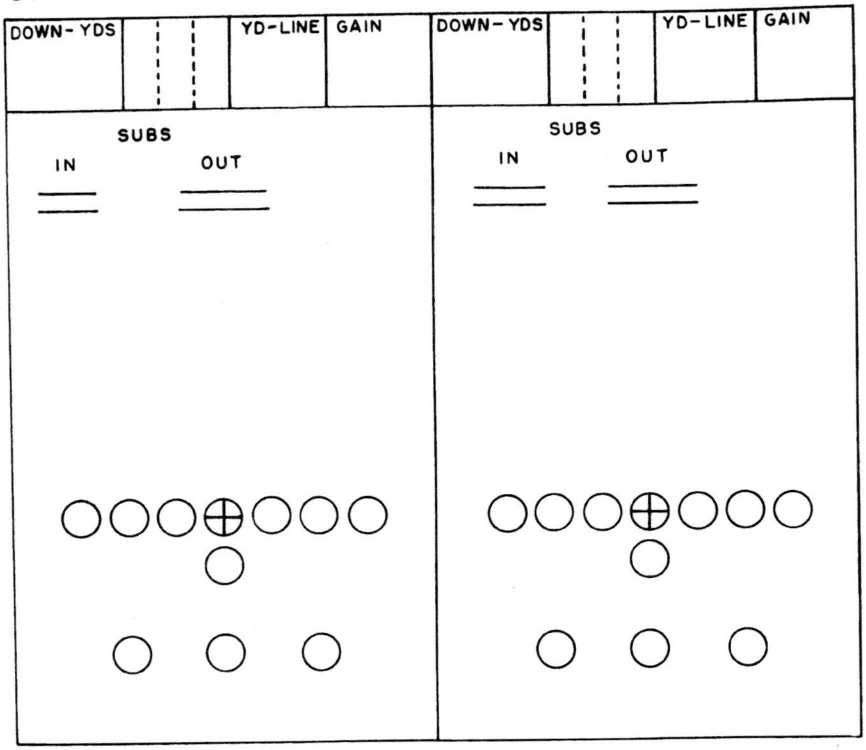

DOWN-YDS			YD-LINE	GAIN	DOWN-YDS			YD-LINE	GAIN

SUBS

IN   OUT

SUBS

IN   OUT

Fig. 4—1. Offensive scouting worksheet.

which shows only that part of the offensive formation that he desires, it is a simple matter to have such forms mimeographed.

Quite often a determining factor in the particular form to be used is the type of offense that is employed by the team being scouted. If a team is primarily a straight T formation team, with little use made of flankers, it seems logical to use a form made up with the entire formation drawn. There will be little need to cross out circles and redraw other circles to indicate the formation. If a team utilizes many flankers, but keeps the ends in tight most of the time, it would be advantageous to omit the half-backs, but to have the offensive line, together with the quarterback and fullback, drawn in. If the formation used on the play differs from that drawn on the form, a personal preference is to indicate the formation with a code or symbols, and then draw in the formation at the conclusion of the game. The only time this would not be done would be when the flanker or split end executed an assignment that was important to the play. Then those assignments would be indicated at the conclusion of the play.

When scouting a team that uses the single wing offense, whether it be balanced or unbalanced line, one of the best and easiest forms to execute is one similar to that partial form shown in Fig. 4–2, with two formations on the left side of the worksheet drawn as single wing left, while two on the right side will be drawn in single wing right. You will use only two of the formations on each worksheet, but time will be saved because there

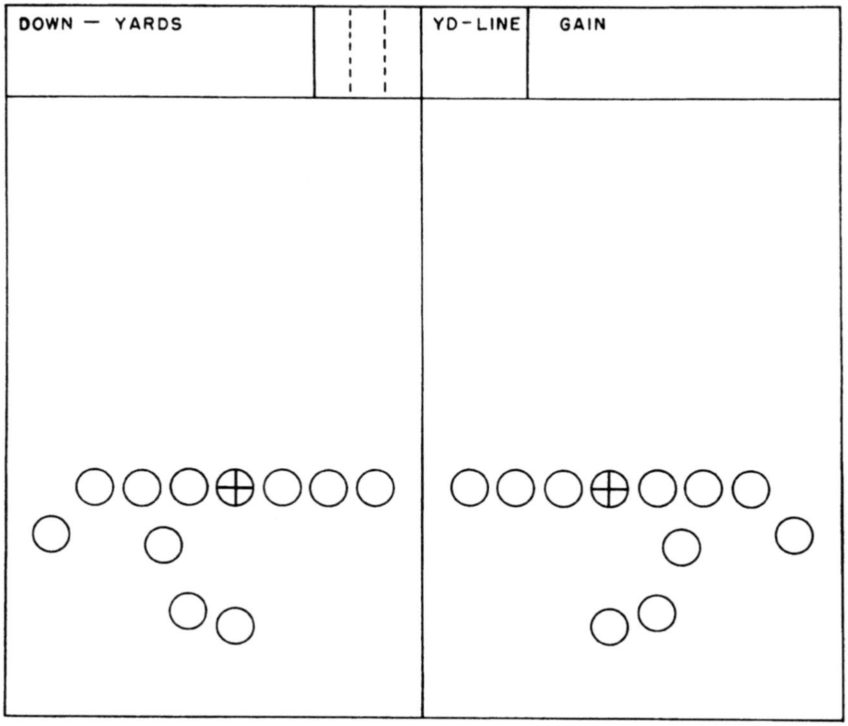

DOWN — YARDS		YD-LINE	GAIN

Fig. 4–2. Single wing scouting worksheet.

will be no need to redraw any circles. The down and yardage to go, the hash mark, and yard line are noted in the proper place. When the team comes out of the huddle and runs the play, the play will be indicated in the place corresponding with the formation from which the play is run.

If so desired, this form can be further changed in the following manner: Two formations are drawn on each page, with single wing right in the top half, and single wing left in the bottom half. The preplay information is noted at the top of the page. When the team comes out of the huddle and lines up in a formation, the proper space is used to indicate the play, together with any pertinent comments. With this system there is but one play to a page, but, as in Fig. 4–2, recording would be facilitated because there would be no need to worry about whether the team would come out in single wing right or single wing left.

Fig. 4–3 shows the top half of a form, similar to that used for the single wing, which can be employed when scouting a team that runs from an unbalanced line and uses the T formation. The form shows, on the right side of the page, the unbalanced line right with the T formation, and on the left side of the page, the unbalanced line left with the T formation. As in the case of the single wing form shown in Fig. 4–2, only two of the four formations on each worksheet will be used.

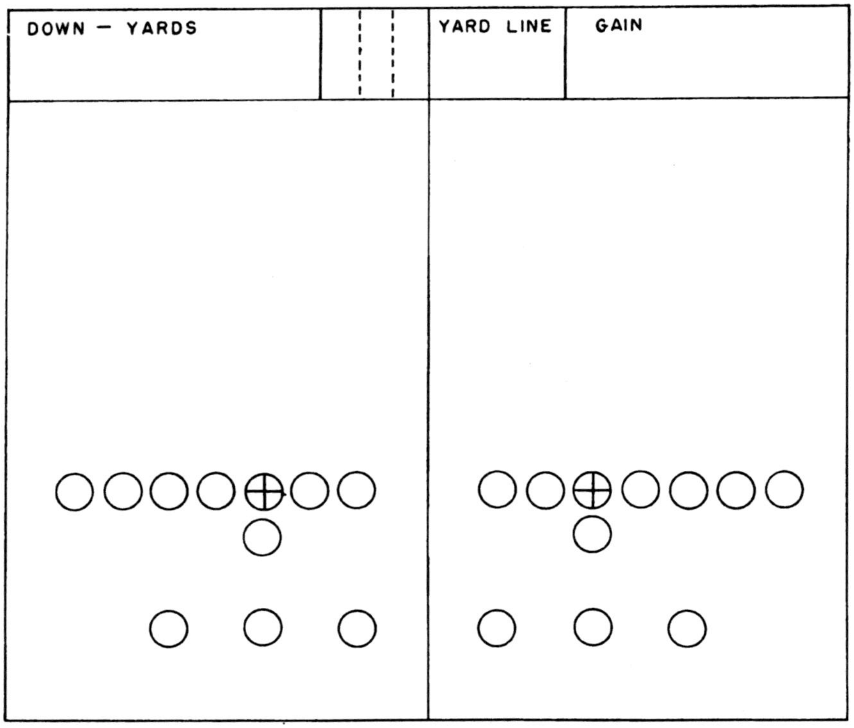

DOWN — YARDS		YARD LINE	GAIN

Fig. 4–3. Unbalanced line scouting worksheet.

Some scouts prefer to use a form that has but one play to a page, regardless of the formation. This allows ample room to draw everything larger, more space for comments or diagrams, and enables the scout to draw anything new or unusual without having to crowd it.

Other scouts like to use their forms, such as the one shown in Fig. 4–1 in the following manner. The upper left-hand formation is used for first-down plays only, and is so indicated. The upper right-hand square is for second-down plays, with the bottom left-hand corner for all third-down plays, and the remaining square for fourth-down plays. Scouts who use this type form will need many more pages to their workbooks. There can be some complications, although there should not be, on plays involving penalties. The point to remember is that every time the team has a first-down situation, you are going to begin a new page. This method has the great advantage of facilitating the compilation of the final form, since you know each square indicates a certain down, and helps you to record many of your down and yardage tendencies much sooner than if other type forms are used.

Still another method of recording the offensive formations and plays is shown in Fig. 4–4. In order to use this form, a scout should have good knowledge of the team that he is scouting, as well as a method of using code letters or numbers to record formations, plays, blocking, and pass patterns. He should also have an easy and understandable method of indicating some of the various defenses, along with the stunts from them.

D-Yds	Fd Pos.	Yd Ln.	Formation	Play	Defense	Gain	Comments
1–10	R	–21	T	27F	54	+4	
2–6	M	–25	4St.	31FQT	W-6	–1	
3–7	L	–24	1Sp.	50 X	W-6	+16	Hit X (1)

Fig. 4–4. Offensive scouting worksheet—code type.

In using a method such as shown in Fig. 4–4, a small pad or tablet should be used as a supplement to show those phases of the game which could not be covered by terminology. These might include pass protection, pass patterns, special blocking, as well as some phases of the kicking game. When something appeared in the game that required additional explanation or diagramming, a number would be put in the space under comments. This would then be drawn in the pad under the same number. An example of this is in Fig. 4–4, on the third play, under Comments with the number (1). The total pattern for that play would be drawn in the pad, since something in the pattern differs from what the scout calls a 50 X.

This particular method is not recommended for the beginner, or even for a scout with limited experience, for use against a team that employs many formations and a varied offense. It could possibly be utilized by a novice against a team that used a limited and simple offense run from very few formations. It could, for example, be used to scout a team that ran the basic Split T, and confined most of its plays to that offense.

Basically, an experienced scout can record as much information using this form as any other, so long as he has a workable code to cover most phases of the game, and a pad to explain the remaining phases. This type form has a great deal of merit for use in "breaking down" films. In either case, whether used in scouting or studying films, it is a very easy form to work with in compiling a final report.

Another type of form that can be used to chart the offense is shown in Fig. 4–5. This form could be especially adaptable for high school use, although it is used on the college level for use in scouting teams that a scout has seen several times and so is quite familiar with the team's offenses and defenses. It can also be used in the off-season, to "break down" movies of future opponents. One sheet is used until completed, or until the end of the quarter, whichever comes first. The same is true of the defensive worksheet as shown in Fig. 4–12 (which is the companion worksheet). In high school scouting, one sheet should be sufficient for a complete quarter. Some of its advantages are: it can be easily handled in a limited work-space, there is little turning of pages, and compilations can be made more quickly. In using a form such as this, it is easier to work with a clipboard, or the method shown and described in Fig. 4–13 of this chapter.

In Fig. 4–5 that part of the worksheet denoted by the figure I is devoted to the offensive play by play. The preplay information of down and distance is shown in the box marked D-D. The yardline is shown underneath in the area indicated with YL. The field position, in relation to the sideline, can be shown by prefacing the yardline figure with the proper descriptive letter. The letters L, M, and R would be interpreted to mean left hash mark, middle of the field, and right hash mark, respectively. The box with the designation Form can be used to show the formation, if it differs from the one drawn in the larger square used to show the offensive play. The result of the play is shown in the space containing the word Gain. If the play that was run can be indicated by a number, this can be recorded above the offensive formation. If the play does not fit into the nomenclature used by the scout, then the play can be drawn. Any pertinent observation can be briefly recorded in this space.

The punt formation can be drawn in the space indicated by the figure II. In the square below, the punter's number can be recorded, along with the distance of the kicks.

Immediately below the punt formation, in Section III of the form, the deployment of personnel for receiving a kickoff, and the kickoff return can be shown.

Section IV of the form is used to show the pass distribution. The approximate area of where the pass was thrown can be indicated by inserting the letters representing the intended receiver so as to denote his position. This section, together with Section V, could be quickly compiled at the

OFFENSE

QUARTER.... SCORE.... ....VS............ ....SCORE.....DATE

D–D		D–D		D–D		PUNT FORMATION
YL		YL		YL		
FORM	○○○○○○	FORM	○○○○○○	FORM	○○○○○○	II
GAIN	○ ○ ○	GAIN	○ ○ ○	GAIN	○ ○ ○	

D–D		D–D		D–D		PUNTER		
YL		YL		YL				
FORM	○○○○○○○	FORM	○○○○○○○	FORM	○○○○○○○	DISTANCE		
GAIN	○ ○ ○	GAIN	○ ○ ○	GAIN	○ ○ ○	KICK OFF RETURN

KICK OFF RETURN
50
40
30 III
20
10
G

D–D		D–D		D–D	
YL		YL	I	YL	
FM	○○○○○○	FM	○○○○○○	FM	○○○○○○
GN	○ ○ ○	GN	○ ○ ○	GN	○ ○ ○

RUN	DISTRIBUTION				
HOLE	DOWNS				TOTAL
	1	2	3	4	
9					
7					
3					
1	VII				
0					
2					
6					
8					
R					
P					

D–D		D–D		D–D	
YL		YL		YL	
FM	○○○○○○○	FM	○○○○○○○	FM	○○○○○○○
GN	○ ○ ○	GN	○ ○ ○	GN	○ ○ ○

D–D		D–D		D–D	
YL		YL		YL	
FM	○○○○○○○	FM	○○○○○○○	FM	○○○○○○○
GN	○ ○ ○	GN	○ ○ ○	GN	○ ○ ○

IV

10 YD   10 YD
○ ○○○○○ ○

PASS DISTRIBUTION

	PASSER		V	
	RECEIVER			
	GAIN			

	LE	LT	LG	C	RG	RT	RE	QB	LH	RH	FB
STARTERS											
SUBS					VII						

Fig. 4–5. A high school offensive worksheet.

conclusion of the game. In the latter section, the passer, receiver and the gain on each pass play can be shown.

A summary of the offense is shown in Section VI. The running game is tabulated by the hole numbers, which are indicated in the left-hand column, while the downs are shown at the top of the space. With each offensive play tabulated in the proper square, an indication can be obtained as to what holes a team may favor on each down. The passing is here summarized by downs, which facilitates uncovering some of the tendencies in passing.

The numbers of the players, according to whether they are starters or substitutes, are shown in Section VII.

How To Develop a Code To Record Special Formations. Regardless of what form is used in scouting, it is important for the scout to develop a simple and concise code to record formations in order to cut down on the amount of writing and charting that would be necessary to clearly indicate the play. If you can develop your own system by abbreviating or simply adapting a code that your staff uses, that is the best. However, many coaches do not use all of the formations that you will see in scouting, and your staff's system of calling formations will generally cover only those formations in your own offense, thus you must improvise or work out a complete system that will cover any eventuality. If a scout doesn't develop a complete system, he must resort to crossing out circles and redrawing others to indicate the various formations. This valuable time could better be utilized in observations and comments about individuals or the team.

One of the most troublesome problems, especially for a beginner, is the development of that part of the code which will easily and clearly indicate flankers, split ends, split backfields, "Lonely" ends, and all the various combinations of these. Once you have decided upon your nomenclature for these maneuvers, abbreviation or coding becomes a relatively simple matter. To help you in forming an easily workable list, some suggestions for the simple calling of rather complex formations will be given.

There are many ways of indicating flankers and various formations. One of the best and easiest methods is the one used at Navy during the 1960 season, and to my knowledge, was one originally developed by Wayne Hardin. Various flanker spots are given a number, as shown in Fig. 4–6.

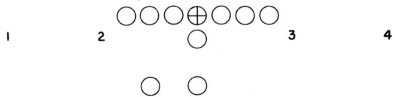

Fig. 4–6. A flanker numbering system.

During the 1960 season, Navy used the same back as a flanker at all times, therefore it was a simple matter to get the alignment desired without the quarterback's having to make a speech. If the quarterback wanted the flanker in any one of the possible positions, he simply called the number designated to get him there. If he wanted a split backfield, the word "split" was added to the number designating the flanker position. A 4 Split formation, for example, is shown in Fig. 4–7.

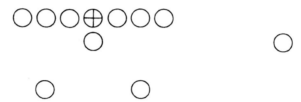

Fig. 4–7. A 4 Split formation.

If the quarterback wanted the fullback lined up in his normal position and a halfback in the right halfback's spot, the word "strong" was added to the number indicating the flanker position. A 4 Strong formation is shown in Fig. 4–8.

Fig. 4–8. A 4 Strong formation.

In order to split an end, the quarterback simply called the end's number along with the backfield alignment desired. In this case the left end is numbered 6 and the right end is number 7. A 4–6 Split formation is shown in Fig. 4–9.

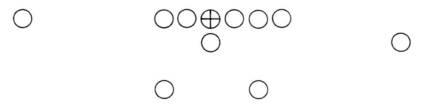

Fig. 4–9. A 4–6 Split formation.

Since Navy flanked only one back, this did simplify the placing of flankers and calling the formation, but this method could be adapted to any system by prefacing the flanking position desired by a letter or number indicating which back should flank. The left halfback could be L, A, or 1; the fullback could be F, B, or 2; and the right halfback R, C, or 3. Then if you wanted to flank the left halfback, the quarterback would call L-1, L-2, L-3, or L-4; or A-1, A-2, A-3, A-4; or if numbers were used, it would be 11, 12, 13, or 14. Should you want to split the backfield, the word "split" would be added to the call made by the quarterback. In this manner, you could get any back you wanted in any flanking position desired. The method previously mentioned of designating a split end is applicable here also, i.e., calling the end's number along with the backfield alignment desired.

There are other methods of denoting flanker positions that are relatively simple. One of these is to speak of flankers as *opposite* or *regular*. If the left halfback is flanked left, and the right halfback to the right, that could be termed an *opposite*. When the left halfback is flanked right, and the right halfback flanked left, that could be called a *regular* flanker. A fullback flanker can be designated as *split right* or *split left*.

If you use only the halfbacks as flankers, another method of indicating the placement of the backs is to preface the call of the side that you want them on by either the word "set" or "flank", depending on which back you want as a flanker. SET LEFT would indicate that the left halfback would go out as a flanker to the left. FLANK LEFT would indicate that the right halfback would be a flanker to the left side. SET RIGHT would put the right halfback to the right, and FLANK RIGHT would put the left half-back to the right.

A great many teams use a halfback in a wing position; this formation can be indicated by simply calling it a wing right or a wing left. Any short flanker that is a yard or a yard and a half outside the end can be referred to by this term, and an abbreviation of WR or WL can be used to record the formation.

Another method of indicating a split end (besides the one previously mentioned of numbering the end) is to name or letter each end. Some coaches call the right end East or Y and the left end West or X. The formation shown in Fig. 4–9, for example, could be recorded in abbreviations as ORSW. Deciphered, this would be: opposite right, split (designating a split backfield), West, i.e., the left end split. The same diagram could also be coded as SRSX, which, decoded, would be: set right, split backfield, and left end split. If you use names to indicate the split ends, you can get abbreviations to cover every situation, including slot formations. Formations can be coded by numbering the flanker positions and lettering the backs, or the procedure can be reversed by lettering the flanker positions and numbering the backs. There are many other methods of denoting these formations, of which those mentioned are but a few.

The methods described of designating split ends can also be applied to a team that uses the "Lonely End" offense. The "Lonely End" formation is indicated by simply adding "over" to the abbreviation or any designation that you have for the end. It could be, for example, LE over, X over, or West over. In reality, it is not the end but rather the tackle that is over, but it gives you the picture of the formation.

Another way of designating the "Lonely End" formation is by using numbers to show the men right of center, those left of center, and the position of the "Lonely End," which is indicated by the digit 1. For example, if the numbers 132 are recorded, this would indicate the "Lonely End" wide to the left, three other men to the left of center, and two men to the right of center. If the code is 231, this would indicate two men left of center, three men to the right of center, and the "Lonely End" out wide to the right.

Similarly, if a team uses an unbalanced line, a simple way to record it is by the use of numbers—indicating the players left of center with the first digit, and those to the right of center with the second digit. For example, the numbers 4–2 would indicate an unbalanced line left, while the numbers 2–4 would mean unbalanced line right. In scouting a team such as the University of Maryland under Tom Nugent, the same system can be used to indicate not only an unbalanced line right or left, but other unusual offensive alignments. Maryland is very apt to, and often has, come out and line up with five men on one side of center and one man to the other side. This has been mixed with a balanced line, a 4–2 and a 2–4 line set. These line variations give a complex picture of formations. It becomes impossible to accurately record all the formations that Maryland might use in one game by marking out circles and adding others to show the numerous formations used.

Numbers can also be used to indicate the relative position of flankers or split ends. If a team varies the distance that the backs are flanked or the ends split, and this information is desired, the distance can be shown by the use of minus numbers for any back or end out to the left, and the use of plus numbers for any back or end out to the right. For example, if you wanted to indicate the left halfback flanked to the left 8 yards, you would record it as L — 8. If you wanted to show him flanked to the right 10 yards, you would indicate that with L + 10. However, if a team uses a multitude of formations, you can hardly expect to get and record distances of flankers and split ends, and still be able to accurately report on the other offensive information desired. You can easily indicate the distance, if a team will occasionally flank one back or split an end.

Sometimes, when this information is deemed important, worksheets are made up with dots placed to indicate 5-yard intervals. Thus, the distance of any split ends or flankers is easily charted, as is illustrated in Fig. 4–10. In the formation shown in Fig. 4–10, the right halfback is set at about 12 yards.

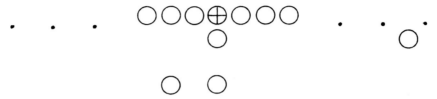

Fig. 4–10.   A method of denoting the split of flankers and ends.

If a scout has to redraw the entire offensive formation, he can, of course, indicate the distance a back is flanked or an end split, by the proper number. Such redrawing of plays should, however, be avoided as much as possible. A code or abbreviations will give you the formation in a few numbers or letters, which is certainly a much quicker and easier way of recording than redrawing plays or crossing out some circles and adding others to the offensive formation already drawn on the worksheet. There are only two possible times to do this, and neither is completely acceptable. The first opportunity is as soon as the play starts. To record a different formation by drawing it at that time means taking your eyes off the team, in which case you are apt to miss part or all of the play. The second opportunity is at the completion of the play, and that takes away from the time that you will have to record observations on the play. By the use of numbers, abbreviations, or some form of code, however, it is possible to record most formations without looking down at the paper. As the formation gets set, you can have your pencil poised on the paper and can write the numbers or letter, and then watch the entire play. It may be that occasionally you will have to draw the formation to show the play in its proper light, but there are many times when an additional number would tell you all that you want to know about the play. One number, for example, could explain the backfield action or the blocking on the line of scrimmage.

DEFENSIVE WORKSHEETS

Basically, the defensive worksheets are very similar to the ones selected to record the offensive play by play. If the offensive worksheet is like that shown in Fig. 4–1, the companion defensive worksheet will likely be similar to that illustrated in Fig. 4–11. The defensive worksheets are also made up with a variety of offensive formations, so the scout can select the one which most nearly conforms to the offense used by the opponent of the team being scouted. If you have no knowledge of the offense used by that team, then a variety of forms should be taken to the game. There are, however, several ways that such information about the scouted team's opponent can be obtained. One suggestion is discussed in the General Instructions in Chapter 3. Another method is for the scout to talk with the head coach or one of the assistants of the team playing your future opponent. This would have to be done several hours before the game, perhaps the day before, since there are few coaches who would want to be bothered by anyone seeking that information just prior to the game. You should explain that you are not asking for any secrets, but that you would appreciate knowing what their basic offensive formations are going to be. Most coaches are very cooperative in giving this information to scouts.

When the offensive and defensive worksheets are very similar in format, there is one change that can be made which will prove very helpful. In order to avoid any mixups in forms during the game, it is advantageous to have the offensive team go "up" the paper in the offensive form, and have the offensive team go "down" the paper on the defensive form. This will eliminate the possibility of confusion, especially when the same type form is used for recording both. An example of such a defensive sheet is shown in Fig. 4–11.

The number of plays that are on each sheet is a matter of the scout's preference. They can be made up from one to four to a sheet. An addition to the form (shown on the right-hand side of Fig. 4–11) which may be helpful is that of horizontal lines drawn in the space that will be occupied by the defensive backfield men. This is to facilitate indicating their depth, and will eliminate having to add the figures of depth for the pass defenders, as you show the adjustments they make to compensate for the various flankers and split ends.

Some coaches will record the defense on a form similar to the form used for the offense, as shown in Fig. 4–4. However, when using this form it is necessary to have a tablet or pad to diagram the defenses that are shown against each formation. A favorite type tablet to use is a regular stenographer's pad. If possible, the formations are drawn before the game, and usually each formation is drawn four times to take care of the eventuality that four different defenses will be used. This system is not recommended for use against a team that employs many formations. If a team has been using three or four formations a game, all formations can be drawn on two pages of the pad. This may be done in the following manner. One formation, as for example a normal T formation, is drawn four times on the first page. On the back of that page, you can draw a Wing Right formation. On the second page, you can draw a Wing Left formation, and on the back of the second page, you can have a Double Wing formation. This is assuming, of course, that these are the formations you anticipate seeing.

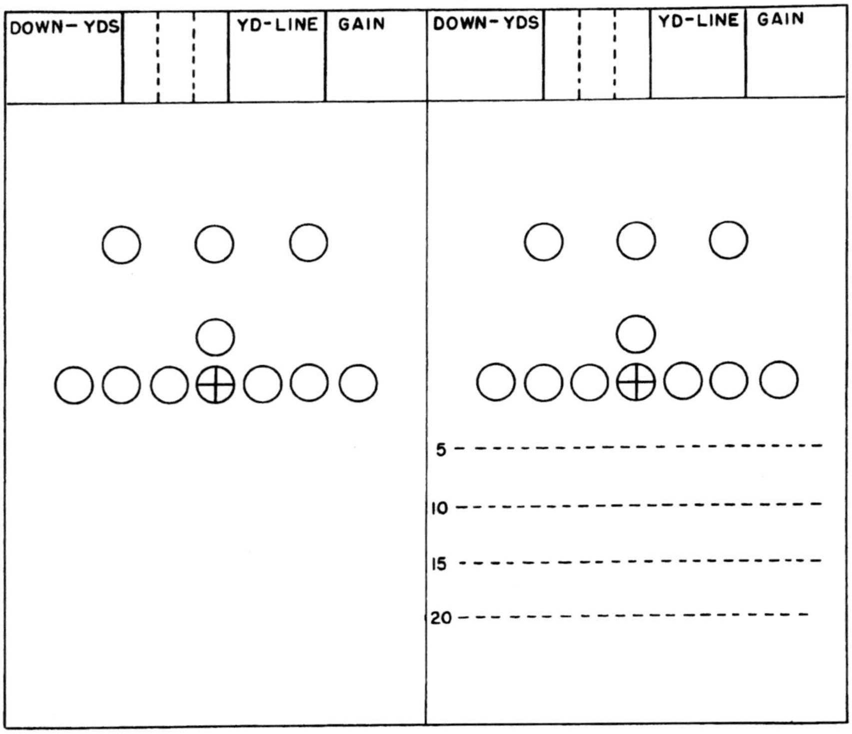

DOWN – YDS			YD-LINE	GAIN	DOWN – YDS			YD-LINE	GAIN

Fig. 4–11. A defensive scouting worksheet.

When the offensive team comes out of the huddle, you determine the formation the team is in, and then look to see what defense is being employed. (The methods discussed in scouting and recognizing defenses as described in Chapter 5 can be used.) At the conclusion of the play, draw in that part of the defense that was recognized. From then on, you may make a mark indicating each time that particular defense is used. If, on another play, the offensive team comes out in the same formation, but the defensive team is aligned in a different defense, that defense will be drawn against the second drawing of that offensive formation. This procedure is followed throughout the game. At the conclusion of the game you have each defense, and adjustments, as used against each formation. This method of scouting and drawing the defense has a great deal of merit, especially for a beginner in scouting, or one with limited experience. You will find that working in this way you will develop a methodical system of observing defenses. Also you will probably get the total defense sooner by using this method, since you are recording it against the same formation every time it appears.

Fig. 4–12 is a sample of another type of defensive worksheet, one which is used in conjunction with the offensive worksheet shown in Fig. 4–5. On the defensive sheet to be used, all the pertinent information can be recorded. In Section 1, the down, distance and the defense used can be indicated in the appropriate space. The different defenses used can be drawn in the spaces shown in Section 2. Information about the kickoff can be noted in Section 3. That part of the game covering the punt rushes and returns can be drawn in the space allotted for that purpose in Section 4. Comments, which of necessity must be brief, on individual players by position can be recorded in the remaining space (5).

If you are using play-by-play charts, as shown in Fig. 4–11, to record the defense, and similar forms to record the offense, it is best to have the forms in one book. Confusion can and will take place if two separate but identical forms are used and are not attached to a notebook in some logical manner. This can be done simply and inexpensively by one of two methods. All that is needed is a soft-covered notebook, or a hard-covered folder, with the fold in the middle. Put two holes on the right edge of the open folder or notebook, so that two small book rings, size 9/16, can be used to hold the worksheets. Put corresponding holes on the right edge of the worksheet and attach with the rings to the folder. On the left edge of the open folder make two holes to attach the other worksheets. On one side of the folder, you will have the offensive set of worksheets, and on the other side you will have the defensive. Both will be attached to the outside edge, which means that you will work the pages from the middle of the folder. As you complete each sheet, you can turn it underneath and out of sight. This arrangement is shown in Fig. 4–13.

Another simple method of having the worksheets in the same folder in an easy working position is shown in Fig. 4–14. Put a couple of holes in the right edge of a folder that has its fold at the top. With corresponding holes in the right edge of the offensive worksheets, attach these with book rings to the right edge of the folder. On the left edge of the folder, also put a couple of holes with corresponding openings in the left edge of the defensive worksheets, and attach to the cover with book rings. Since both sets of worksheets are attached at different ends by book rings, it is a simple matter to put on top the ones that you are working with. When the team is on offense, you slip the offensive sheets to the top and work with them until the team gives up the ball and goes on defense. You then slip the defensive worksheets on top and work off them as long as needed. Regardless of whether you are working with offense or defense, as you complete a sheet you turn it underneath, and it is out of sight as well as being out of the way. If desired, it can be turned as a page in a book, and the back can be used for notes.

It has been found much easier and more convenient to use worksheets

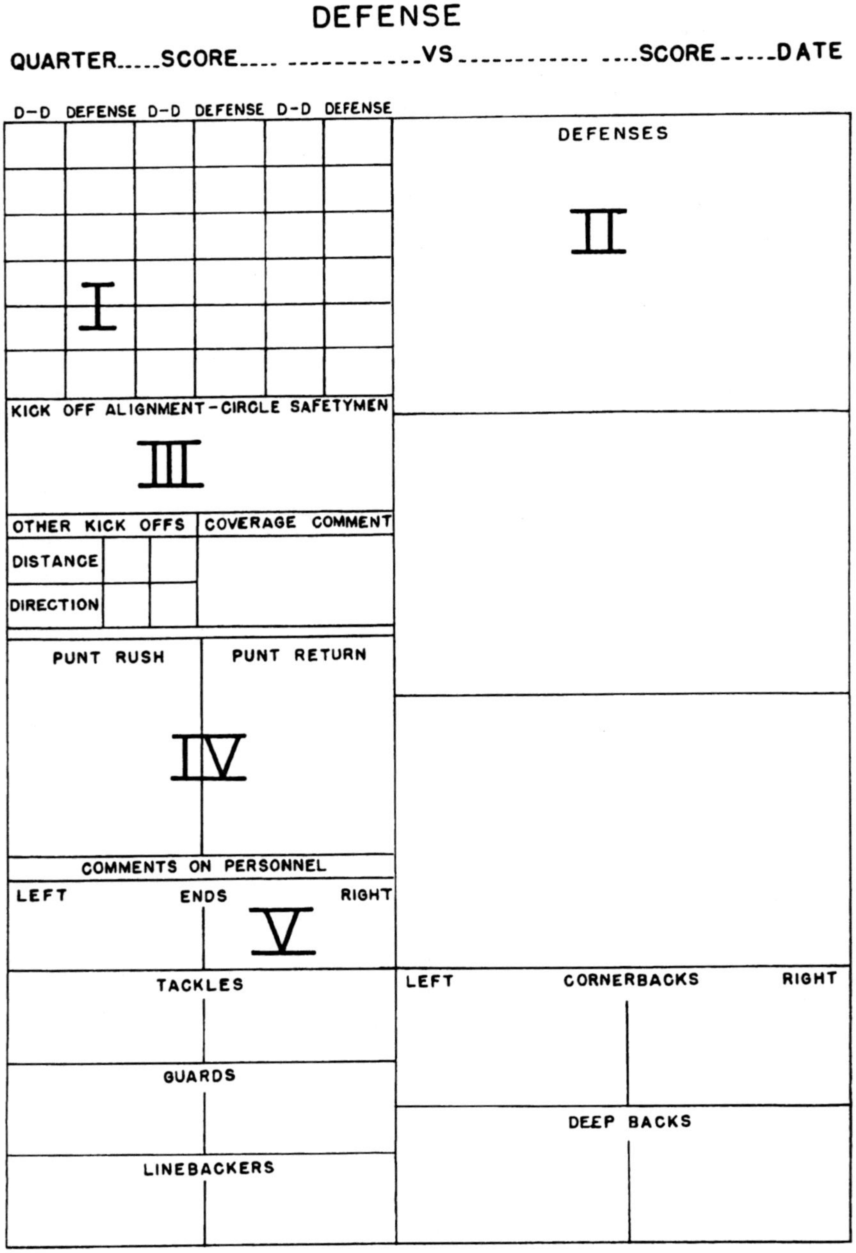

DEFENSE

QUARTER.....SCORE.... ....VS............ ....SCORE.....DATE

D-D DEFENSE D-D DEFENSE D-D DEFENSE

	DEFENSES
I	II

KICK OFF ALIGNMENT-CIRCLE SAFETYMEN

III

OTHER KICK OFFS	COVERAGE	COMMENT
DISTANCE		
DIRECTION		

PUNT RUSH	PUNT RETURN
IV	

COMMENTS ON PERSONNEL

LEFT	ENDS	RIGHT
	V	

TACKLES	LEFT	CORNERBACKS	RIGHT
GUARDS		DEEP BACKS	
LINEBACKERS			

Fig. 4–12. A high school defensive worksheet.

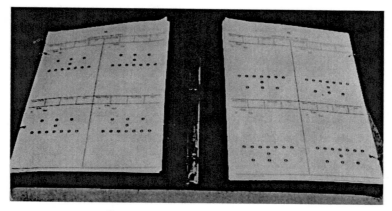

Fig. 4–13. A scouting workbook.

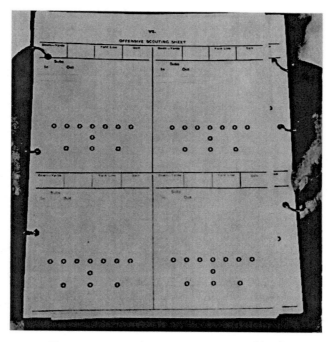

Fig. 4–14. Another type scouting workbook.

that are kept together with book rings, than those that have staples to hold them. Staples restrict the freedom of the papers, and it often becomes difficult and cumbersome to use them after quite a few sheets have been used and folded underneath. Rings of any type give you an even surface to work on, as well as convenience in turning pages after you have completed them.

Regardless of what forms you decide to use, make sure that they are the ones that you like the best, and can help you do your best work. The less shuffling of forms, pads and papers that you have to do, the better off you are. Your situation as to the place you have to sit to scout ball games should help you decide which forms best suit your needs. Many high school coaches, for example, do not have the facilities of a press box, so it is imperative that they have forms to work with that are easy to handle and give them convenience, satisfaction and results.

TERMINOLOGY

Although a scout may choose his forms, his terminology must be the same as that used by the other members of his coaching staff. In order that there may be conformity in terminology among the members of a staff, a terminology list should be prepared. This list should cover as many terms as necessary. There are numerous ways of indicating the same thing in football, and it is essential that everyone speak the same language. The importance of all coaches using the same nomenclature can be readily appreciated by any coach who was a member of a staff where, if uniformity existed, it was only by accident. Unquestionably, most staffs will have a list of terms to cover the more obvious and prevalent phases of the game. But in many cases the list should be expanded to include many more terms, so that valuable time will not be wasted in misunderstandings, but will be used to advantage in coaching.

The following example is a partial list of some important terms, and the meaning they have for a particular coaching staff.

Jack Blocking. Both guards pull on a play off tackle or around end.
Boom Blocking. Only the far guard pulls on a play off tackle or around end.
Pitch Blocking. The near guard pulls on a play off tackle or around end.
Switch Blocking. The guard and tackle cross block at the point of attack.
Change Blocking. The tackle and end cross block at the point of attack.
Crackback. A flanking back or split end comes back in to block a defensive man to his inside.
Sweep. An end run in which the quarterback hands the ball to the ball carrier.
Toss. The quarterback tosses the ball to the ball carrier on a sweep.
F. The backfield maneuver in which the fullback fakes up the middle, and a halfback carries the ball off tackle or around end.

H. The backfield maneuver in which the halfback fills for a pulling guard on a play off tackle or around end.

On-side. That side of the line through which the play is being run.

Off-side. That side of the line away from which the play is being run.

Near Back. The back closest to the point of attack on a sweep or off tackle play.

Far Back. The back farthest away from the point of attack or point of discussion.

Flanker. Any back that is aligned in any flanker position.

In Back. Any back that is aligned in his normal T formation position.

Split Backs. Backs that are aligned in the normal halfback positions with no one in the fullback spot.

Wing. A back aligned approximately one yard outside of either end.

Slot. A split end with a back flanked to his inside.

W-6. Wide 6 defense in which the tackles are aligned over the offensive ends, and the linebackers over the offensive tackles.

5–4. The Oklahoma 5–4 defense.

Rotated. The defensive backfield went from a two-deep alignment to a three-deep on a defense that would normally be a two-deep defense.

Four Deep. The cornerbacks on a two-deep defense drop back to the approximate depth of the deep men.

Prevent. The defensive backs get back to a depth of 15 or more yards late in the half or late in the game, in order to prevent a long touchdown pass.

Plugger. A linebacker that shoots across the line of scrimmage in a pre-determined move to stop the play on the offensive side of the line.

Chugger. A defensive man that attempts to keep an offensive man from getting downfield as a pass receiver.

Swing. A back that runs a pass pattern parallel or near parallel to the line of scrimmage until he gets outside the defensive end, and then heads up field.

Flare. A back that runs a pass pattern slightly inside or outside the defensive end to a depth of about six to eight yards, and then breaks over the middle.

Banana. A back that runs a pass pattern inside or outside of the defensive end to a depth of about six to eight yards, and then breaks for the sideline approximately parallel to the line of scrimmage.

Stop. A flanking back runs downfield in a pass pattern, stops and turns toward the passer.

Hook. An end does the same thing that a back does on a "stop" pass.

An example can be cited to show the value of uniform terminology to a scout and the members of a staff. In scouting a game, a scout could record a play and understand what took place from a notation as follows: 29F-J-CB. This would mean that the No. 2 back carried the ball through the nine hole. The backfield action incorporated a fake by the fullback up the middle. Both guards pulled to lead the play, and there was a crack back block by the split end or the flanker back. The scout would know who was involved in the crack back block by referring to the formation from which the play was run. This same terminology could be used in recording the play in the final report, and every member of the staff would know what took place without the use of any diagrams or explanation.

In addition to the list of terms used by his staff, a scout may need to compile a list of terms of his own. These can be a great timesaver in recording the observations of a team being scouted. It can also be advantageous to a scout to be familiar with the terms used by other coaches. Otherwise, when he seeks information by discussion with other coaches and other scouts, much time can be wasted in reaching a common understanding of many terms. A scout should have, and continually further develop, a list of terms and expressions that can be used to explain, describe or name different actions in football.

5

How To Recognize the Defense

It is much easier for the average beginning scout to recognize offensive formations than defensive alignments. Special attention, therefore, is directed to the problem of recognizing the various defenses. In order to quickly and accurately record the defense on the worksheet while the game is in progress, a scout must be able to *instantly* recognize defenses as soon as they appear. There will be no time for the scout to waste in figuring out the defensive alignment. Each scout knows what he should look for, but too often he (especially the beginner) does not know how to look for the information which will quickly indicate to him the total defense that he wants to record. Even an experienced scout can learn to speed up his recognition of the total defense so that he will have more free time to spend in observation of individual players.

One of the easiest and quickest ways to identify a defense is by the rapid observation of two separate defensive groups: (1) the backfield alignment, and (2) the interior defensive players on or near the line of scrimmage. This can be accomplished in two quick "looks." The partial picture (actually, the identifying part of the defense) so obtained by the scout as a result of two "looks" will be referred to here as the *defensive count*. Once the scout has ascertained the defensive count, he can quickly determine the total defense and record it immediately.

To get the defensive count, the scout should train himself to look at the defense in the following manner. The first look should be at the defensive backfield to determine whether it is in a two- or three-deep alignment. Many times the first look can be taken as the offensive team comes out of the huddle. If this is the case, then the scout can immediately concentrate his efforts on the second look to get the defensive count of the interior line. If, however, the defensive backfield alignment is not set as the offensive team comes out of the huddle, then it must be observed when the defense is set. A look at the defensive backfield plus a look at the interior defensive players, regardless of deployment, will pretty much tell you the total defense. The important factor in these "looks" is to first get the defensive count that all defenses will have.

STANDARD DEFENSES

For example, in Fig. 5–1, with two quick looks the defense is recognized as an Oklahoma 5–4. The deployment of only seven defensive players has been established, but the total defense is fairly evident. There are but a limited number of alignments that could be taken by the remaining defensive players, and still present a fundamentally sound defense.

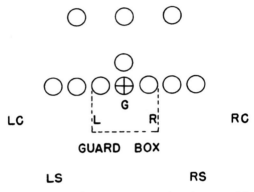

Fig. 5–1. The defensive count within the guard box.

The defensive count shown in Fig. 5–1 would be 1–2–2. The first digit indicates that there is one man head on the center, on the line of scrimmage, between the offensive guards. The second number represents those players off the line of scrimmage who are over any part, or to the inside of the offensive guards. These players represented by the first two digits will be referred to as those inside the guard box. The deep backs are given the third number, in this case 2, to represent their two-deep alignment. The quickest and surest way to establish the first number of the defensive count is to look to the offensive guards to see if they are "covered," i.e., if there is a defensive man head up on or to the inside of each of them. It is better to check the offensive guards to see if they are covered rather than to see if there is a man head on the center, since by the latter method a gap odd defense might not be recognized—i.e., an odd defense where the middle guard moves over into one gap or the other, between the center and guards, and leaves the center uncovered, thus giving the impression that it is an even defense when only the center is checked.

After getting the defensive count, it is a relatively simple matter to determine the total defense by looking to the defensive players deployed to either side of the defensive count (ends and tackles). These should be observed not as individuals, but as two other groups. In a series of four rapid looks, two to get the defensive count, and two to place the remaining players on either side of the defensive count, the total defense is quickly recognized. With practice and concentration, these looks can be taken so quickly that it actually seems as though you are getting the total defense with one look.

If the scout has experience and can adequately observe an area that encompasses more players than those which have been referred to as within the guard box, then he can think in terms of getting the first two numbers of the defensive count by also including the players on or to the inside of the offensive tackles, i.e., those within the tackle box. Fig. 5–2 shows a

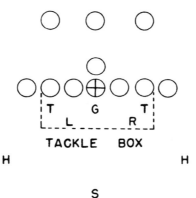

Fig. 5–2. The defensive count within the tackle box.

defensive count of 3–2–3, obtained by observing those players within the tackle box. Thus with two looks he can set eight of the defensive players. With this defensive count, the scout can readily recognize the total defense and record it on his worksheet in his own nomenclature, such as an Oklahoma 5–4 rotated, or an overshifted 6 man line.

To further explain the use of a defensive count to help quickly determine the total defense, some of the more prevalent defenses used in football will be diagramed. Diagrams will show the two possible defensive counts, one showing the count of players within the guard box, another those players within the tackle box. The scout can choose, according to his ability and experience to determine the defensive count by confining his observations to either the guard box or the tackle box. After getting the defensive count, whether obtained from the guard box or the tackle box, the scout observes the deployment of those players to either side of the defensive count to complete the total defense. The important point, and this cannot be stressed too strongly, is to get the defensive count first, and then work from there to get the total defense.

Fig. 5–3 shows the defense commonly referred to as a 6–1, with with-out backfield rotation. The defensive count within the guard box of the defense shown on the left would be considered a 2–1–2, while the defensive count within the tackle box as shown in the defense on the right would be considered a 4–1–3 count. In the former count you have established the alignment of seven defensive players, since a two-deep situation will in-dicate to you that there will be a cornerback to either side of the twin

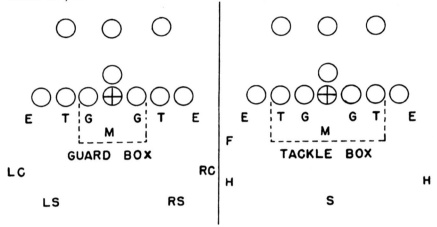

Fig. 5–3. The defensive count of a 6–1 defense.

safeties. In the latter count you have established the alignment of eight defensive players, and in many cases can quickly place the ninth man (the other defensive back) as the offensive team comes out of the huddle. In either case, in several quick looks you can get the defensive count and the total defense.

The importance of being able to encompass more area in one look is shown in Fig. 5–4. The defensive count within the guard box and that within the tackle box are shown. The example on the left could represent the defensive count of four different defenses, whereas that on the right could represent the defensive count of only two defenses. The defensive count within the guard box would be 2–0–3, and would fix the placement of five defensive players. This could represent the defensive count of a 4–4, a Wide 6, a Tight 6, or an 8–3 defense.

On a 4–4 defense, the linebackers would be off the line of scrimmage over the offensive tackles, the defensive tackles over the offensive ends, and the ends to the outside off the line of scrimmage the approximate depth of the linebackers. On a Wide 6 defense, the alignment would be the same as for a 4–4, with the exception of the ends who would play on the line of scrim-mage. On a Tight 6 defense, the defensive tackles are over the offensive

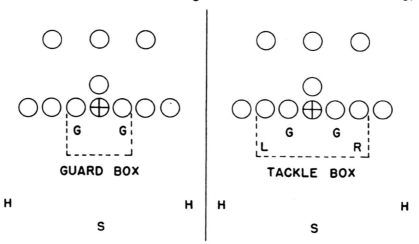

Fig. 5—4. The defensive count of a Wide 6 defense.

tackles, the linebackers over the offensive ends, and the defensive ends are to the outside of the offensive ends on the line of scrimmage. An 8–3 would be easily distinguishable because there would be no linebackers.

The defensive count from within the tackle box as shown on the right would be 2–2–3. Seven defensive players are shown, and the picture of the total defense is fairly complete. The defensive count would be that of either a 4–4 or a Wide 6 defense, and which one could easily be determined by a look to either side of the defensive count.

The defensive counts in Fig. 5–5 show a count of 0–2–3 in the example on

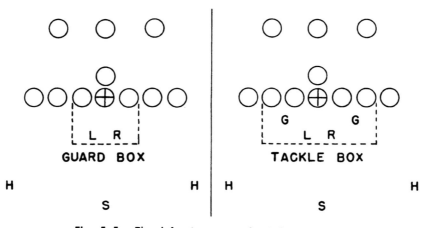

Fig. 5—5. The defensive count of a Split 6 defense.

the left, and a count of 2–2–3 on the right. It is evident that the defense is a Split 6. The only remaining problem is to determine the alignment of the players to each side of the defensive count. In this case the possible alignment of the players outside of the defensive count is quite limited.

Fig. 5–6 shows a stacked defense where the count is the same regardless of whether you take the defensive count within the guard box or within the

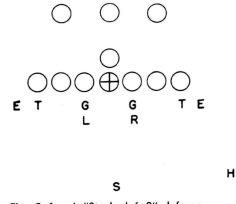

Fig. 5–6. A "Stacked 6–2" defense.

tackle box. In both cases with two looks at the proper areas you get the placement of seven of the defensive players. This defensive count is 2–2–3, which helps identify the defense as a Stacked 6.

In Fig. 5–7 you can see a defensive count of 1–1–3 (within the guard box) or a 3–1–3 (within the tackle box), depending on the size of the area the scout has the ability to adequately observe. Both of these defensive counts could represent either a 5–3 or a 7–1 defense. The areas outside of the defensive count must be observed to finally determine the total defense.

In Fig. 5–8 two versions of a 4–5 defense are shown against an offensive formation with a flanker. In the defense shown on the top you would get the same defensive count, 2–1–2, regardless of whether the count was taken of those players within the guard box or those within the tackle box. However, in reality more information is obtained from the tackle-box defensive count, which indicates that the linebackers are probably stacked, and this would help identify the defense as a Stacked 4–5. In the other alignment of the 4–5 defense, shown on the bottom, you would get a defensive count of 2–1–2 within the guard box, which would show only that it is some form of a 4–5 defense. The 2–3–2 count within the tackle box, however, would indicate to you that this is not a *Stacked* 4–5 defense, since the linebackers are included in this defensive count. This is another example of the advantage of the scout's working to broaden his scope to include the larger

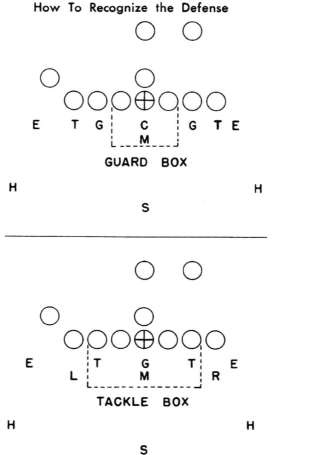

Fig. 5–7. The defensive count of a 7–1 and a 5–3 defense.

area of the tackle box, rather than confining his observations to the guard box.

The Eagle 5–4 could possibly present two different defensive counts within the guard box, depending upon the alignment of the tackles. If the defensive tackles were on the outside shoulder of the offensive guards, the count would be the same, 3–0–3, taken within the guard box or within the tackle box. Fig. 5–9 shows the tackles playing wider, however, and thus changing the defensive count. It would then be a 1–0–3 count within the guard box, but a 3–0–3 count within the tackle box. The total defense could be obtained from the guard-box observation, but the defensive count of the tackle box would make the quick recognition of the total defense easier.

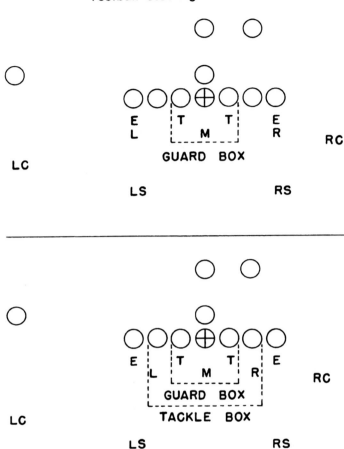

Fig. 5–8. The defensive count of a 4–5 defense.

SHORT-YARDAGE DEFENSES

Short-yardage defenses are a special case and should receive special treat-
ment. Since it is a relatively simple matter to identify the defense as a
short-yardage seven- or eight-man line by a look at the defensive backfield,
your attention should be focused on the alignment and charge of the players
on the line of scrimmage, rather than on obtaining a defensive count.
Generally, a short-yardage defense will be used less often than other defenses, and the maximum detailed information should be obtained the first
time a short-yardage defense is observed. You must determine not only
how many players are deployed on the line of scrimmage, but also whether
they are playing head on or in the gap—and their charge.

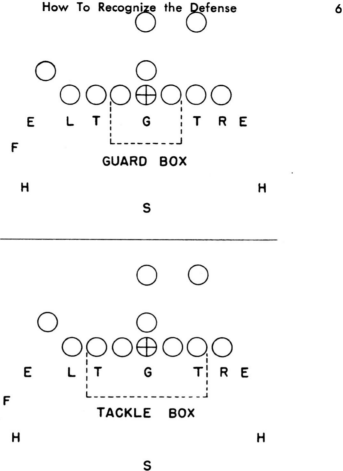

Fig. 5–9. The defensive count of an Eagle 5–4 defense.

The quickest and easiest way to determine the responsibilities of the men on the line of scrimmage is to observe three internal defensive men on one side of the offensive center. (Binoculars can be very helpful in this particular observation.) Such a "look" will show whether the defensive linemen are lined up head on or in a gap. If they are lined up in a gap, their only really effective charge is into the gap. If they are lined up head on, however, the charges of one guard and the two defensive linemen to his outside are scrutinized. Such scrutiny will show if the linemen are hitting head on, if they are hitting the inside gap, or if they are hitting the outside gap. If the same defense is observed a second time, the opposite guard and the two defensive men to his outside should be similarly scrutinized.

In a head on alignment when there is a middle linebacker, sometimes a combination of defensive charges is used, such as shown in Fig. 5–10. The guards are hitting the inside gap, while the rest of the linemen to the outside of the guards are hitting the outside gap.

Fig. 5–10. A short-yardage or goal line 6–1 defense.

DEFENSES AGAINST AN UNBALANCED LINE

Often a problem arises for the scout when, because of his concentration on the defense, he fails to recognize the formation when the offensive team surprisingly lines up in an unbalanced line. This could also be caused by a lack of proper procedure, inexperience, or lack of training in being able to recognize the offensive formation before scouting the defense. Even when a scout has a wealth of experience, an unbalanced line is often difficult to quickly identify if a team employs a variety of offensive formations, including split ends and all types of wide flankers. In most cases, the defensive team becomes aware of the change in offensive alignment and adjusts its defenses accordingly. The adjustments from a defense facing a balanced line to one facing an unbalanced line will show up quickly in the form of some unusual defensive counts, when the scout has failed to observe the unbalanced line.

After looking at the defensive backfield, a scout's natural inclination is to look at the man centering the football, considering him to be the apex of the area the scout will scrutinize to get the defensive count. When using this method, the beginner has a tendency to more or less disregard the other offensive linemen not aligned in the immediate area observed. If he does this, and thus overlooks the offensive unbalanced line formation, his defensive count will be a very unusual one. This should alert him to the possibility that he has missed an offensive change to which the defense has adjusted.

When the team you are scouting defensively is playing against a team using an unbalanced line, the procedure used to get the defensive count may be altered in one respect. The apex man offensively will generally be the middle man of the offensive line, that is, the guard to the strong side of the line, rather than the offensive center. In most cases, when a defensive team is confronted with an unbalanced line, the defense will adjust by over-shifting the line and linebackers one offensive man to the strong side. This defensive adjustment will give the linemen and linebackers the same basic responsibility that they would have in playing against a balanced line. This action by the defensive team will make the middle man, rather than the center, the apex man of the offensive line. There are times, however, when the defensive team will not overshift the line and linebackers to meet this added strength by the offensive team, but will compensate for the unbalanced line by rotating the defensive backfield. This adjustment by the defensive team will necessitate taking the defensive count from the offensive center. This latter adjustment would be possible from what would normally be a two-deep defense such as the Oklahoma 5–4, a 6–1, or a 4–5 defense. Unless such rotation took place, it would be most unusual, and the soundness of the defense questionable, if a defensive team did not play the middle man of the offensive line as the apex man—when the defense was in a standard two-deep alignment. The normal three-deep defenses such as a Wide 6, a Tight 6, or a Split 6 would also have the strong-side guard as the apex man.

Since, when confronted with an unbalanced line, there is an exception as to who may be the apex man in obtaining the defensive count, both possibilities will be considered here. When the defensive team is in a two-deep alignment, the defensive count will be taken from the middle man of the offensive line. You get the defensive count by observing the deployment of the defensive men on or to the inside of the three middle players (those within the guard box), or the placement of the defensive players on or to the inside of the five middle players (those within the tackle box). The scope of vision will again depend on the capabilities or the desire of the scout.

When the defensive team being scouted is in a three-deep defense and you know the offensive team is using an unbalanced line, continue to use the middle man of the offensive line as the basis for obtaining the defensive count. If, however, when doing this you are confronted with some strange and unusual defensive counts, then use the offensive center as the apex in obtaining the defensive count. It could be that the defensive team is employing what would normally be considered a two-deep defense, but has rotated the defensive backfield into a three-deep alignment.

Often a defensive team will adjust some defenses which are normally considered two-deep to an offense that employs a balanced line, but splits an end wide, in much the same manner that they would adjust those same defenses to an unbalanced line. The adjustment by the defensive team is to overshift the line and linebackers one offensive man to the side of the tight end. To compensate for this overshift the defensive backs are rotated to the side of the split end. This action by the defensive team can often confuse the offensive team, as well as some of the scouts observing it. With this adjustment the defense can present two completely different pictures. The defensive count of the overshifted defense would be an unusual one, and an unusual count should alert the scout for an adjustment. An example of the difference in the defensive count between what is considered a normal Oklahoma 5–4 and the same defense overshifted is shown in Fig. 5–11.

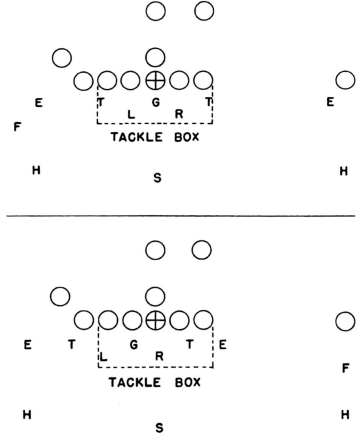

Fig. 5–11. The defensive count of a normal and an overshifted 5–4 defense.

Fig. 5-12 shows examples of three defenses drawn against a balanced and against an unbalanced line. Those on the left indicate a normal defensive count within the tackle box of a defense played against a balanced line.

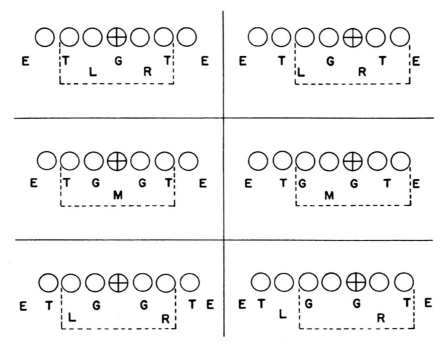

Fig. 5–12. The defensive count of defenses against a balanced and an unbalanced line.

Those on the right show the defensive count within the tackle box of the same defenses played against an unbalanced line, which was not recognized, and therefore the count is based on the offensive center as the apex man. If the scout sees unusual defensive counts such as these, he should be alert for offensive formations to which the defense has adjusted.

The defensive count is also used to advantage when you are scouting a team that frequently changes its defenses while the offensive team is at the line of scrimmage. In most cases players will move from one predetermined spot to another. Usually for every move made by one man, there is a compensating move made by another—in reality, there is a change in responsibility between the players involved. These moves are generally a short distance and usually involve linebackers. More often than not, such moves include players in the defensive count and are therefore under close observation by the scout and help him to detect such stunts. Whereas stunting does not normally affect the defensive count, it is vital information which should be carefully noted in the play by play.

Since a team can get quite involved in defensive stunts, it is imperative that a scout have a way of recording them. His method should be relatively simple, but he should be able, through code or abbreviations, to accurately explain the defensive stunt. One method that has proven very satisfactory will be discussed. In Fig. 5–13 the numbering and lettering of the different players is shown. This can be applied to the simple and quick recording of most defensive stunts used in high school or college football.

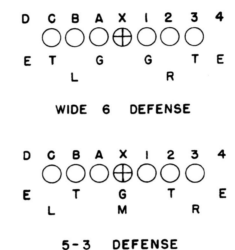

Fig. 5–13.   A method of designating players to indicate defensive stunts.

The right side of the offensive line is lettered in the following manner: right guard, A; right tackle, B; right end, C; and wide to the right, D. The center is indicated with an X. The left side of the offensive line is numbered 1 through 4. Defensively, the left linebacker is indicated with L, the middle linebacker with M, and the right linebacker with R. When the linebacker is involved in a stunt, you have a simple way of showing what might well be a complicated maneuver by merely indicating which linebacker does the stunting and which offensive hole is his new responsibility.

Fig. 5–14 shows some examples of defensive stunts from a Wide 6 defense. Each side can stunt independently of the other side.

Fig. 5–15 shows some defensive stunts from the Oklahoma 5–4 defense.

In Fig. 5–16 there are some examples of stunts from both a 5–3 and a 4–5 defense. In both cases they are the same type stunts, but from a different alignment.

The whole theory of calling the stunts this way is, in reality, very simple.

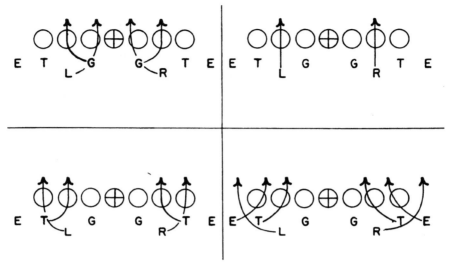

Fig. 5–14. Defensive stunts from a Wide 6 defense.

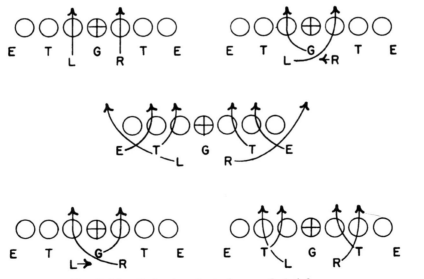

Fig. 5–15. Defensive stunts from a 5–4 defense.

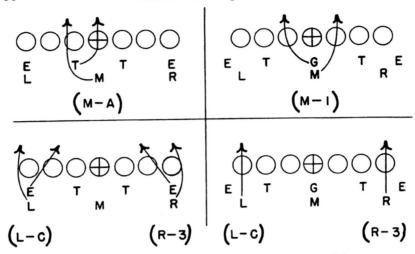

Fig. 5–16. Defensive stunts from a 4–5 and a 5–3 defense.

You indicate which linebacker is stunting through which offensive man. If there is a defensive man over that offensive man to begin with, the defensive man is going to move to a position on the snap of the ball that will enable him to assume the linebacker's previous responsibility, or move to another position that, along with the move of the linebacker, will keep the defense sound. Even should there be some slanting by the linemen, such can be indicated, as well as where the linebacker shot. This is shown in Fig. 5–17.

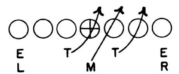

Fig. 5–17. A slant right M–1 stunt from a 4–5 defense.

THE "INDISTINGUISHABLE" DEFENSE

There are times when a team will line up in a totally unfamiliar defensive alignment in which it is difficult to distinguish the placement of the internal linemen and the defensive count. When confronted with this, a scout will usually wince and wonder where to start to decipher the defense. After the first look to the defensive backfield, the approach found to be the easiest for the author is to begin by observing the players on the immediate inside of the end men, i.e., the second defensive men in—whether they be linebackers or linemen. Mentally, note the position of the two outside or end men. As soon as the alignment of the four outside men is established, on the first play if possible—if not, on the second—look to the interior linemen. Start with the inside and work out, placing first the men on either side of the ball. If you get that part of the defense that you can usually see the clearest, the outside men, you will be able to put the rest of the defense into place much quicker. This is the only time that the author feels that you should not begin by working from the interior line out. Unusual defenses can be distinguished much faster this way than if the usual approach is used.

During the 1957 football season, Navy used several defenses that fell into this category, and they were difficult to scout. Additional confusion resulted when the players would "jitterbug" and change their responsibilities. One of these defenses is shown in Fig. 5–18. By using the method just described,

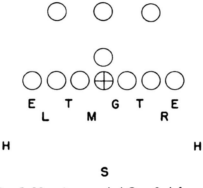

Fig. 5–18. A concealed Gap 8 defense.

the alignments of defenses of this type are not as difficult to determine as it first appears. The linebacker on each side is in the gap between the tackle and end. The ends play head up to the offensive ends, of which the scout should make a mental note. With the defensive backfield set, you have now determined the alignment of seven of the eleven defensive players. By then turning your attention to the inside men, you can establish that one man on the line of scrimmage is in the gap between the center and guard, and one linebacker is in the gap between the center and other guard. Nine of the eleven men are now placed, so it can be assumed, until confirmed, that the tackles are also in the gap. As the scout observes this defense develop, he can identify it as a concealed Gap 8.

This defense was sometimes altered to give a different picture, but basically it was the same defense. The variation was accomplished by having the middle linebacker and the gap defensive guard exchange gaps. One outside linebacker and the tackle on that linebacker's side would also do the same thing. This gave the alignment shown in Fig. 5–19.

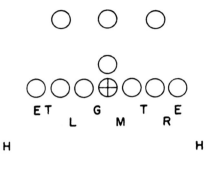

Fig. 5–19. A variation in alignment of Fig. 5–18.

The defenses shown in Figs. 5–18 and 5–19 are, however, highly irregular. Through trial and error and the use of many different approaches, the method of using a defensive count to determine the total defense has been found the most satisfactory for normal situations.

In addition to identifying the alignment of different defenses, the scout will also need to watch for various movements of the individual players. That phase of scouting the defense will be dealt with in the next chapter.

6

Scouting the Defense

PREGAME OBSERVATIONS

In order to do an effective job of scouting a team, it is imperative that you get to the game in ample time and be fully prepared. Allowances should be made in case delays are encountered somewhere along the line. Naturally, it is better to be there early and have time to spare, rather than arrive late and possibly miss part of the game.

You should be in your seat and ready to observe the players when they come out for their warm-up. This is a good time to get your first impressions of the specialists. You can observe the punters to check their kicks for distance, type of kick and the number of steps that they take in kicking the ball. If the information is desired, you can use a stop watch to determine the amount of time that each punter takes in getting off a kick. This is an excellent time to notice how well the centers can snap the ball back to the kickers, and this might be the only time that you can see each of them do this. If any one of the centers has any trouble, make a note of it, since it is possible that even if he isn't a regular he may have to play against you, as a result of injury to other centers. It is wise to note the distance that the kickoff men are able to kick the ball. One of the important observations that should be made is who kicks the extra points, as well as who kicks the field goals, and of special note is the distance that these men can kick. During the 1959 season, in an important ball game, a team fell victim to a fake field goal attempt from the 32 yard line. This would have been a 42 yard kick, and it could have been observed in pregame warm-ups of that and previous games, that the kicker's maximum range was from the 25 yard line.

Much worthwhile information can be obtained from watching the passers. Among the things to look for in a passer are: how fast he sets up to pass, how deep he sets up, and—of great importance—how far he can throw the ball. You might also note whom the passers are throwing to and on what type of patterns. You will often see receivers running what might well be their favorite patterns; this is particularly the case when there is a faking or a timing element involved. This seems to be especially true of a team that emphasizes the passing game.

It is questionable whether you should come to any definite conclusions on all your observations of the specialists in pregame workouts, but these observations could help to substantiate something that is seen in the game. On the other hand, players (and especially punters) will often do much better in practice than they will under pressure of a game. The threat of what they *can* do, however, should not be overlooked.

Not all of the scout's time should be devoted to watching the specialists, as it can be helpful to observe the linemen as they loosen up in their various drills. If you see guards pulling out and heading upfield, it seems logical to expect them to do this in the game on some plays. The same thing holds true for the tackles. A team that does any slanting or looping on defense will usually have the linemen make a few of those moves in their pregame work.

This period can also be a good time for the scout to get down close to the field to get the quarterback's cadence at the line of scrimmage. In many of the warm-up drills used, the signal callers will use the regular cadence. If a scout is working alone, this might well be his best opportunity to get the cadence. Should two or more scouts be working the game, one of them can go down as close as possible to the field late in the half or near the end of the game to ascertain the snap count.

Quite often in college football today, injuries are not publicized, but by close observation it is possible to determine whether any key members of the team have any injuries. Very frequently the trainer or one of the coaches will closely watch one of the players warm-up, to see if he is capable of the maneuvers that will be expected of him in the game. This knowledge could have some bearing on the game, since a player who cannot operate at full efficiency might be vulnerable defensively, while ordinarily he might not be. An injury to a key man could, of course, affect the offensive play of the individual as well.

In order to adequately observe the pregame warm-up of a team, the use of binoculars is highly recommended. The numbers of the players can be seen and recorded much sooner. It is also possible to get a closer look at individual movements. Pregame warm-ups can often supply helpful additional knowledge to the scout. It definitely is not a time to just idly sit by and wait for the action to begin.

GAME ACTION

1. KICKOFF. Most scouts will get the kickoff alignment by working from one sideline to the other as they record the numbers of the players. Before the ball is kicked, note whether it is to be kicked from the hash mark or the middle of the field. The type of kick and its distance can be information of value since it could affect the return that your team would use. As the ball is kicked, try to determine the approximate distance of the kick as quickly as possible by immediately looking to the spot where the probable receiver is waiting to catch the ball. It is important not to simply follow the ball all the way down the field, since very little of the coverage can be observed if this is done. Try to focus your attention on the coverage as soon as possible, and it is important not to watch individuals, but rather try to look at the entire coverage to see if, as the team moves downfield, any openings are created either as a result of one or more men's being slow or individuals not covering in their proper lane. If you detect an area that appears weak, you can concentrate on that spot on the next and succeeding kickoffs, and perhaps establish a vulnerable lane that your team could take advantage of. As the teams unpile, record the numbers of those players who were in on the tackle. On a subsequent kickoff, you might check to see how fast they get down under the kickoff. This could affect the kickoff return that your team will use.

As you follow the team down under the kickoff, you can usually determine what player or players act as safety men since they will generally cover very slowly, or they will go downfield fast for 10 or 15 yards and then slow up. It is essential that you get the coverage, so it is possible that you will watch just the start of the kick, and then concentrate your attention on the coverage. Most coaches want to know whether the kicking team does an adequate job of covering the sidelines as it comes down, who the contain men are, and whether they converge quickly and make themselves vulnerable to an outside return.

If two scouts are working the game together, there should be a distinct division of responsibility on the kickoff. One scout can call off the alignment as the other records. Here, too, binoculars are very helpful in quickly establishing the numbers of the players. On the actual kickoff, one scout can cover one side of the line, with the other scout observing the remaining side. To appraise the coverage, one scout can watch the kick and then follow the receiver to see how far he runs before initial contact is made by a defensive player. (This can be important in determining how soon the receiving team should start throwing its blocks on the return.) The other scout can watch the general coverage.

2. DEFENSIVE PLAY BY PLAY. While the offensive team is in the huddle, record on your defensive play by play the down, the yardage to go for a first down, and the position on the field, both horizontal and vertical, i.e., the yard line and position in relation to the sideline. In recording the yard line, it will be much easier to refer to it by a plus or minus sign. If the ball is on a team's own 10 yard line, for example, simply record it as on the −10.

If it is on the opponent's 10 yard line, mark it as being on the +10. Often the beginner will have difficulty in recording all the preplay information as the team huddles, because he is still doing a lot of writing about the last play and doesn't get started soon enough on the present one. This is one important reason why a scout should make wide use of abbreviations, numbers, or a code that he understands. However, when difficulty is encountered, it can be minimized if, on first down, the scout will carefully indicate the down, the yard line, and the gain on the play. In the next square indicating the next play, he marks 2—for the second down—but he can omit the distance needed for a first down and the yard line. The same applies to the third and fourth downs. In order to use this short-cut method, it is imperative that all information be recorded on first down, and that the yardage gained or lost be shown after each play. At the completion of the game the other figures can very easily be filled in before the scout starts the analysis of the play-by-play account.

While the offensive team is huddling, it should also be noted whether the defensive team shows the defense before the offensive team breaks the huddle. Since the defense is right on the ball, it often occurs that after getting the defensive signal the team will get in its approximate alignment while the offense huddles. This happens quite often and it should be duly noted when it does, as this knowledge could be beneficial. (It would then be a simple matter for your quarterback to look up and see what defense would confront him on the next play.) Many teams will do a good job of camouflaging the intended alignment of the defensive line, but the defensive backs will usually get in their positions for the next defense before the offensive team comes up to the line of scrimmage.

As outlined in the previous chapter, a scout can learn, with concentration, practice, and the right approach, to recognize the predominant defenses used in football today. Since most teams use but a few defensive alignments, it should be but a matter of a short time until you distinguish them in a series of quick glances. The sooner that you can establish what the defenses are, the more time you will have to devote to looking for the play of individual players, or the adjustments of those defenses that are used. One of the first things that you may want to note (if your head coach requests such information) is the adjustment and rotation to various flankers and split ends. In order to get this information, it is imperative that you recognize the offensive formation and know which back is flanked. The quickest and most accurate way to get the formation is to first watch the offensive team come out of the huddle to see if an offensive man is sent wide to a flanker position. If it is established that there is a flanker, look to the backfield to determine whether it is a strong or cross flanker (left halfback set to the offense's right or right halfback set to the offense's left), or if it is an opposite flanker (right halfback set right or left halfback set left). This must be done quickly so the scout can look to the defense and get the defensive count, the total defense, and finally the adjustments that are made. All that is seen must be committed to memory until the play is over, then it should be noted on the worksheet. If a short abbreviation, a number, or a code is used to record a formation, the pencil can be poised to write it in the appropriate space at the time you see it, but it is important that you do not take your eyes off the playing field. If rotation and backfield adjustment is important to you, it is urgent that you note it at some time during the ball game, and the sooner the better. If need be, you may have to get the rotation and backfield adjustment at the exclusion of some other information, if this phase of the defense must be covered in your report.

When two scouts are working together, the responsibility must be divided. One good method is to have one scout assume the definite responsibility of getting the defensive count; the other scout should get the alignment of the remaining defensive players. If the first scout is doing the recording, the second should also get the offensive formation. If the offense employs any type of flanker, he should observe the defensive adjustments on the side of the flanker (because that is the side where most defensive adjustments will take place). The first scout should observe the play of that side of the defense away from the flanker. It is obvious that a simple method of recording flankers and split ends is essential in order to keep up with the pace of the ball game. Once the scouts know what the defense does against each type flanker employed against them, then they should start looking for detail in individual alignment and play of those affected by the flanker. When the offensive team does not employ a flanker, then each scout should have a definite predetermined responsibility for observing the defense. In order for both scouts to get a complete picture of the defense, the responsibilities can be exchanged at the end of each quarter.

DEFENSIVE PERSONNEL

1. GUARDS. As the game progresses, you will begin to recognize the defenses in a series of glances and you can begin concentrating on the various players in each defense used. You can start with the play of the middle guard on an odd defense. It can be helpful to know whether he lines up on the ball or two feet off the ball. If he is playing off the ball, insert a figure to denote how deep he is playing. Does he play "soft" when he is off the ball and play "tough" when he is right up on the ball? Does he use his hands on the offensive center, or does he hit him with a forearm? If he uses a forearm, which one? This is important because he is practically helpless against a double team block from the side that he uses a forearm. Regardless of how he plays, it is imperative that your center work against a defensive man using that same method of play. You should check to see if the middle guard ever drops out of the line to get into pass defense. This can be determined by noting the number of men that rush the passer, or by the number of men on pass defense. Among the other things about the guard's play that can be noted are whether he ever shoots the gap, or if he ever slants. You can easily tell whether he plays high or low.

On an even defense, it is important to know the guards' depth, what their alignment is and what their charge is. Do they play a "soft" game, or are they trapable by virtue of a hard charge? In checking the play of the guards on an even defense, or of the middle guard on an odd defense, it is important to check them on different yardage situations, since their play will generally differ on a third-and-one situation from their play on a third-and-twelve.

2. TACKLES. In scouting the play of the tackles, much the same pattern as that for the guards will be used. You will want to note their depth and the various charges that they employ   If the team is using the Oklahoma defense and there is any stunting or dealing between the tackle and the linebacker on his side, what is forthcoming usually can be detected by checking the feet of both the tackle and the linebacker. Their alignment and the position of their feet will often give them away. (This kind of tip-off will be covered more fully in a subsequent chapter.)

When there is stunting by a tackle with an end, the tackle will quite often give it away by getting deeper. This is generally true on a Wide 6 defense where the tackle is playing head up to the offensive end, and, of course, the defensive end is to the outside. One of the favorite stunts from this defense involving the tackle and end is to have the end smash hard down the line of scrimmage off the tail of the offensive end, and have the tackle cover the outside. This is often used in this defense as an effective change of pace. Many tackles, however, will telegraph their moves by getting a little further off the ball than usual, to insure their getting to the outside without getting cut off. Many will also change the position of their feet to execute this maneuver. For example, a left defensive tackle that is used to having his right foot back when playing a normal Wide 6 defense, will find it rather difficult to take an outside charge with his feet aligned that way. If, on another charge, he is called to drive down on the shoulder of the tackle, it is practically impossible to do an effective job when the left foot is staggered to any noticeable extent. In observing any defensive linemen, make special note of those that you see who have either foot with a big stagger. A lineman who does have a big stagger is limited in his charge in that the offensive man playing opposite him knows that his opponent's first step has to be with that back foot to get any power in his charge.

On a play away from the tackle that you are observing, notice if he is the leverage or chase man, and how well he does his job. This means that he has the responsibility of taking care of any play that should start away from him and then come back to his side in the form of a naked reverse or a Statue of Liberty type play. The important point here is to see how deep he gets across the line of scrimmage.

3. ENDS. In checking the play of a defensive end, it is important to observe whether he plays close enough to the offensive end to be hooked, and thus would insure the effectiveness of an end run when that type of blocking was used against him. Some coaches want to know if the defensive end is in a two- or three-point stance, and which foot is back. If he plays in a three-point stance, indicate it with an E, while if he is in a two-point stance, indicate that with ∧ (an inverted V). Of more importance is the manner in which he plays his position. Does he play along the line of scrimmage, or does he penetrate? If he penetrates, does he go straight across the line of scrimmage, parallel to the sideline, or does he go across on an angle? If he does go straight across, he could make the off-tackle hole more inviting, since it is easier to block out an end who penetrates in that manner, and run inside of him. If he comes across on an angle, it should be more effective to hook him with a back and run wide. It is important to know if he gets into the pass defense by dropping back and covering the flat when a pass shows. Again, you should check the style of play on different yardage situations. You should also see how effective he is at rushing the passer. Could he be vulnerable to a screen pass? Another important point to determine is how far out will he go with a flanker?

4. LINEBACKERS. In observing the play of the linebackers, there are undoubtedly more things to look for than at any other defensive position. How well your team can handle the linebackers can determine to a large extent how your team will fare against the opponent. Their depth from the ball and the mobility that they possess are of great importance. If, for example, on the Oklahoma 5–4 defense, they are up close to the line of scrimmage and are not deeper than the feet of the middle guard or tackle, you will quite often find that they are not really effective on outside plays. They are often forced to take a deep angle of pursuit, rather than find themselves able to pursue along the line of scrimmage. When they are in this position you will seldom see them stunting with another defensive player. They will however "shoot" from this position, and can be very effective. It is generally difficult to run trap plays up the middle when the linebackers play close. If they vary their depth, check to see if there is a reason for it. Of course, most linebackers will naturally align themselves deeper on an obvious passing situation. If a linebacker is favoring the side of the tackle in lining up, look for some stunt involving the linebacker and tackle, or the linebacker, tackle, and end. If a linebacker favors the middle guard in his alignment, look for a stunt involving those two players.

If the linebackers are fast and active, it is important that your guards work against linebackers who give that picture. The guards will have to take a good route to cut the linebacker off by getting between him and the point of attack. If the guards are taught to fire out at the linebackers, regardless of the point of attack, they must learn to keep their feet and block the linebackers past the hole.

It is important to try to establish on whom the linebackers key. Most linebackers will key on the offensive lineman in front of them, but some will key on the quarterback, others on the flow of the backfield, and in some cases will key on an individual such as the fullback or a halfback. Quite often you will find when the linebackers line up fairly deep, they will be keying on someone on the offensive team other than the offensive linemen right in front of them. When the linebackers are right up in the line or close to it, generally they are keying on the offensive linemen or are up there to shoot. Regardless of what the key of a linebacker might be, he will eventually go with the football, and the speed with which he can do this distinguishes the good one from the rest.

Another point that you will want to check concerning the play of the linebackers is the speed with which they get to their pass defense responsibility. The relationship of their speed to that with which the deep backs get their depth can be important. If the linebackers are slow, and the deep backs fast, then there is going to be an open area between the linebackers and the deep backs that cannot be covered by either. What angle do the linebackers take in going back to their hook responsibility? Some will take a very sharp angle and thus leave a large open area between the two linebackers. Others will go practically straight back and make it more inviting to throw in the flat. Do they ever cover a swing or flare man? If you are associated with a passing team, it is vital that you find out the answers to as many of these questions as possible. If forward passing is not an integral part of your offense, then this information could be of little value, and your time could be better spent on checking things that would be more beneficial to your team.

If your team employs split ends and flankers, it is important to note what, if any, adjustments the defense will make to these offensive variations. Since 1957, Navy has never run from a conventional T formation with no flankers. There has always been one back flanked, and usually an end split on the side away from the flanking back. In scouting for Navy, it is important to note the defensive deployment versus all flankers and split ends. The adjustments are going to affect, to some extent, the offensive planning, and they certainly can affect the blocking to be used. The adjustments could differ in each defense used, and if this is the case, it is imperative that such adjustments be noted carefully.

5. DEEP BACKS. The play of the deep backs should be scrutinized for many details, since a weakness in their play can be exploited for long gains or touchdowns more easily than a weakness in play at any other position. Among the things that you should observe of the deep backs are their depth, adjustment to flankers and split ends, alignment, and coverage. If they play exceptionally deep, then it is likely that you will have to try to complete passes in front of them. If they play shallow, seven yards or less, it is not always necessarily true that you can complete passes beyond them. It is imperative to check their reactions as soon as the ball is snapped. (This does not mean that it has to be a pass play for you to check this.) If the deep backs do not move, or take a step backward on the snap of the ball, it might be difficult to get a receiver beyond them. If, however, they take a step or two forward at the start of the play, they might well be fooled by a play-action pass. This would not necessarily be true at all times, since some backs are exceptionally good at keying and recognizing the difference between a pass and a running play. However, those that key and recognize plays well are in the minority. On a drop back pass some defensive backs retreat so rapidly that it is often easier to pass short in front of them. They are going back so quickly that they find it difficult to stop quickly and react to a pass thrown in front of them.

The coverage is probably of the greatest importance insofar as the deep backs are concerned. Most college and high school teams use some type of zone defense, but there are teams that use a man for man, or a combination man for man and zone pass defense. Before the ball is snapped, you can usually get a good idea what type pass defense a team is utilizing, if the opponent makes any use of flankers. The adjustments made by the deep backs will generally tell you whether they are playing a zone or man for man defense. In a three-deep defense, if the halfback moves out head on the flanker and the safety man moves over to a position head on the offensive end to the side of the flanker, they are undoubtedly playing man for man pass defense. This is shown in Fig. 6–1. If the safety man stays about head on the offensive center, they undoubtedly are playing a zone defense. Of course, in either case coverage should and can be verified by observing the deep backs on a pass play. It must be remembered that if the ball is on or near a hash mark, and the flanker goes to the wide side of the field, on a zone defense most safety men will move over and favor the wide side of the field in order not to give that defensive back too much territory to cover to the wide side of the field.

When a team is in a two-deep defense, there are some tip-offs to look for to see whether a team is employing a zone or man for man defense. If a flanker is set out and the corner man drops off to the approximate depth or equal to that of the safety man on his side, they are in all probability play-

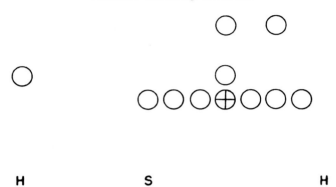

H   S   H

Fig. 6–1. The backfield adjustment on a three-deep defense
on man-for-man coverage.

ing man for man defense, as shown in Fig. 6–2. This is the alignment of a
two-deep defense versus a flanker when man for man coverage is used.

If the corner back widens, but maintains a depth of approximately half
or less of that of the safety men, they are probably playing a zone defense.

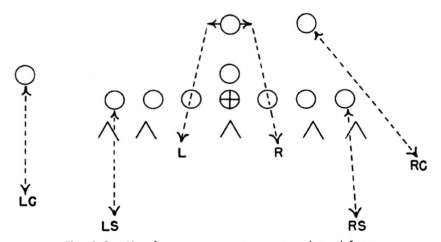

Fig. 6–2. Man-for-man coverage on a two-deep defense.

Usually when they present this picture, a team will revolve into a three-deep
zone defense on the snap of the ball. The best way to verify this is to watch
the deep safety man away from the flanker. If, on the snap of the ball, he
goes into the deep middle, you can be sure that it is a zone defense. The
safety man would go into the middle on a drop back pass or a roll out toward

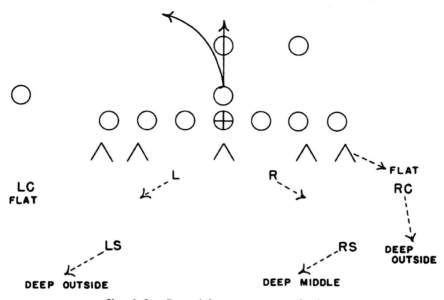

Fig. 6–3. Zone defense rotation to flanker.

the flanker, as shown in Fig. 6–3, which illustrates the alignment of the defensive backs and their pass defense responsibility in a camouflaged three-deep zone. This would be one type of coverage for a drop back pass or a roll out action toward the flanker.

If the play developed into a roll out action away from the flanker, the revolvement could be reversed with the corner back on the flanker side taking deep outside (opposite the direction of the roll out), the left safety on the side of the flanker would take deep middle, and the right safety, away from the flanker and on the side of the roll out, would take the deep outside in the direction of the roll out. The cornerback away from the flanker would take the flat zone. These are the zone defense responsibilities from a two-deep alignment (a camouflaged three-deep) on a roll out pass away from the flanker, as shown in Fig. 6–4.

Regardless of what type pass defense is being used, it is important for the scout to indicate where passes are being completed against a team, and what defensive back or backs are involved in the completions. Any time that a receiver gets beyond a defender, whether the pass is completed or not, this should be duly noted. By the same token, it should also be noted when receivers try to get beyond various defenders, but are unsuccessful in doing so.

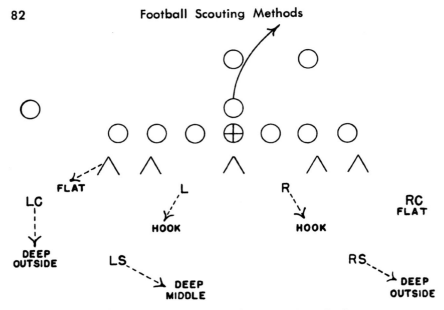

Fig. 6—4. Zone defense rotation away from flanker.

It must be remembered that a scout is not going to see all that he would like to see at a game. In observing the defensive actions, concentrate on those that will be of most importance to your staff in helping to formulate game plans.

7

Defensive Analysis

There are many approaches to the preparation of the defensive portion of the final scouting report after seeing a team in action. It is logical, however, that the scout should first make a thorough study of the different defenses that were used before he attempts to make any analysis of where and when each particular defense was employed. It is important to know each player's alignment on each defense, what each player's responsibility was, and the adjustments made to each type of flanker. Rather than drawing the defenses in the order that they were used in the ball game, the scout will find it easier to learn each defense if he takes the defenses in the order of their importance and completes the study of the first before going on to the next one. For example, if a team used a Wide 6 and an Oklahoma 5–4 as its basic alignments, first draw the one that was used the most. Show the alignment of all players, the charges that they took, their responsibilities, and all the adjustments to the different offensive formations. All the stunts from this defense should also be drawn. If possible, each defense with all the variations should be shown on one sheet or card so that all phases of that defense can be seen without having to thumb through several pages. Then the same should be done with the next most prevalent defense, and so on through all others that were used by the team being scouted.

Underneath each defense, or on an attached sheet or card, comments should be written about the play of each individual player. The strength and weakness of each player should be duly noted, and such comments on the strength and weakness should cover those appraisals precisely and should not be statements of a general nature that are of no value in game preparation. For example, to say that No. 82 is an average football player in reality tells you nothing of any consequence. It is more helpful to say that No. 82 is very strong against wide plays, or that he is weak on power plays at him, or some such statement of a concrete nature that can be used to help formulate game plans. These statements should be as brief as possible, but to the point.

A sample report of one of a scouted team's defenses will follow. Fig. 7–1 shows the way the team lined up in the defense. The discussion and explanation of the play of the individual players follows. The comments here do not deal with any of the substitutes, but in making an actual report, all players that were observed by the scout should be discussed.

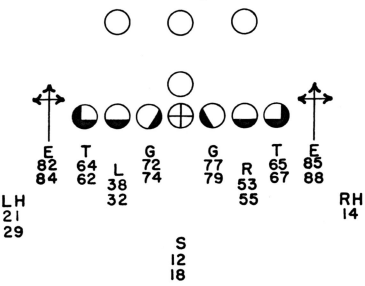

Fig. 7–1. The alignment, responsibilities, and personnel of a Wide 6 defense.

GENERAL NOTES. This was their alignment in the W-6 defense. It was their favorite defense in this game. With all variations and stunts they were in this alignment thirty-two times in this game.

PERSONNEL:

Guards. They play the offensive tackles as defensive guards. They will vary their alignment from on the ball to two feet off the ball. When on the ball, played head up with the offensive guards, but very inside-conscious. Did not move out when offensive guard split wide. Not very agile or quick, but very strong. It would be difficult to run inside of them on straight plays or traps. They could be "logged." (This means that since they are so inside-conscious the trapper could hook the defensive man, rather than try to block him out. The ball carrier must then divert to the outside of the hole called. In order to do this successfully, both the offensive guards and the ball carrier would have to practice this adjustment.) When the defensive guards are off the ball, they either will play "soft" or will stunt. Neither defensive guard was effective rushing the passer. They were piled up in the middle most of the time. Would be vulnerable to draw plays to their outside. Never saw either one get into the pass defense.

Tackles. The offensive guards play as defensive tackles. Will play on the ball or about two feet off the ball, head up or to the inside of the offensive end, depending upon the split. If head up, will hit end and take outside. If inside shoulder or inside gap, they will charge out and try to control the end. Both defensive tackles are very quick and agile. Will play off the ball if stunting with either the end or the linebacker. Each defensive tackle is a leverage man. (This means that the tackle will have the responsibility of any naked reverse or delayed plays coming back to his side after starting away from him.) Number 65 is tough on plays right at him, but can be trapped. The left defensive tackle, No. 64, is by far the best defensive lineman. Very difficult to block, and plays traps well. Both defensive tackles do an excellent job of rushing the passer.

Ends. They play about 2 yards outside the offensive end in a three-point stance. They step across the line and react to the play. Number 82 plays wide plays well, but can be blocked out on off tackle plays. Does excellent job covering the flat on pass defense. Number 85 appeared very weak on wide plays. Played off tackle hole well. Slow getting into pass defense. The ends will work with the defensive tackles in holding up the offensive ends on long-yardage situations. They were very effective in doing this. Both ends will drop off into the flat on drop back passes. They will force roll out action toward them, and drop off into the flat on roll out action away from them. Number 82 is best all-around end.

Linebackers. Line up head on the offensive tackles, clearing the feet of the defensive linemen. Both linebackers pursue well. Number 38 is not strong on plays run at him. Number 53 is exceptionally tough, and best defensive football player. Both linebackers get to hook responsibilities well. On roll out action both go fast in the direction of the roll out, leaving the off side hook area wide open. Both linebackers will cheat when stunting.

Halfbacks. Play 8–10 yards deep and about 4 yards outside the offensive ends, and play straight zone defense. Number 14 is defensive specialist. Both come up very fast on running plays and are excellent tacklers. They can both be fooled on play passes, but No. 14 is especially vulnerable. No pass receiver has gotten beyond either one on drop back or roll out pass. They get back fast after pass is recognized. Appear to be vulnerable on stop or hook passes about 12–15 yards deep. Both have good speed.

Safety. Plays 10–12 yards deep and offers poor running support. Is the best pass defender, and it is doubtful that he could be fooled on play-action pass. Gets back very fast on drop back action. Is vulnerable on passes in front of him. Does not like body contact. Has excellent speed.

ADJUSTMENTS:

Ends. They did three different things versus wide flankers. They played their normal end position, went out to a head on position with the flanker,

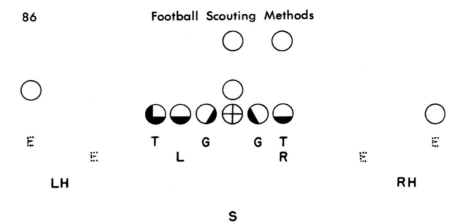

Fig. 7-2. Adjustments versus flankers and split ends from a Wide 6 defense.

or played in a walk away. (The latter term means that end would drop off the line of scrimmage and split the difference between the flanker and the next offensive man to the inside.) Got into pass defense from any of these alignments. Against a split end, they played head on up to about 8 yards. If the split was more than this, they played in a walk away position.

Linebackers. The only adjustment made was on the split end side when the linebacker would get directly back of his tackle and get 3–4 yards deep.

Halfbacks. Played same depth and widened some, but were 3–4 yards to the inside of wide flankers and split ends. Vulnerable to stop outs or hook outs. They made no noticeable adjustment to a wing on either side when the wing was about one yard wide.

STUNTS. The different stunts used from the Wide 6 defense are shown in Figs. 7–3, 7–4, and 7–5. In Fig. 7–3 the defensive guards would be off the ball about two feet and the linebackers would cheat in enough to be noticed. Did this against any formation.

In Fig. 7–4 the defensive tackles lined up a little deeper, and they would hit the offensive end and go to the outside. They did not do this on the

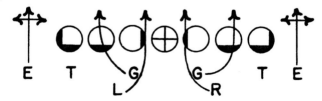

Fig. 7-3. "LA" and "R-1" stunt from Wide 6 defense.

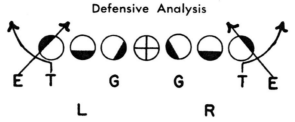

Fig. 7—4. "TD" and "T-4" stunt from Wide 6 defense.

side of a split end or a short flanker. Each side did this independent of the other side.

In Fig. 7–5 the linebackers would cheat out a little so as to make sure that they got to their responsibilities. They did not do this to the side of a short flanker or split end.

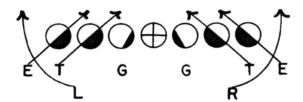

Fig. 7—5. "LD" and "R-4" stunt from Wide 6 defense.

Now, having finished with your information on the Wide 6, you should proceed to similarly treat, in the order of their importance, all other defenses seen in the game.

When each defense that was seen in scouting a team has been diagramed, explained, and commented on, an analysis should be made to see if it can be determined what defensive tendencies a team may have. From the defensive play by play, there is often much information that can be detected through careful and diligent analysis. Nearly every football team has some defensive tendencies—the extent of these tendencies will vary from team to team. It may be that you cannot establish when a team is going to use a particular stunt, but you can recognize certain situations when that team will stunt. There are also definite times when a team will not stunt. Field position will often be a determining factor as to when a particular team will begin to use stunting defenses. Other teams will stunt at any place on the field, and it is important to have this information. Whether or not a team employs stunts as part of the defensive plan, the team is surely going to believe that certain defenses are better to stop an anticipated running play, while others are considered stronger against passing. It should not be difficult to determine what a team uses for a short-yardage or goal-line defense. However, in order to uncover the total defensive thinking of a team, a systematic analysis should be made.

One of the first things you will need to know is what defenses were used on various down and distance situations. There are several ways this information can be obtained from the defensive play-by-play. One form that can be followed is shown in Fig. 7–6. Each defense used in the game is

DEFENSE			DEFENSE			DEFENSE			DEFENSE			DEFENSE			DEFENSE		
L	M	R	L	M	R	L	M	R	L	M	R	L	M	R	L	M	R

DEFENSE			DEFENSE			DEFENSE			DEFENSE			DEFENSE			DEFENSE		
L	M	R	L	M	R	L	M	R	L	M	R	L	M	R	L	M	R

Fig. 7–6. Defensive analysis sheet.

indicated in the space under Defense. As the scout goes through the defensive play by play, he records the down and distance for each time that defense was used—in the appropriate hash mark space. This form will show what defenses a team favored on certain down-and-yardage situations, and is obviously especially good for showing hash mark tendencies. For example, it will show which defense was favored on first and ten, as well as on the various long- and short-yardage situations. Since the defenses are recorded according to field position, it will show if the team does or does not favor stunting certain players on certain parts of the field. Often a team will favor stunting players on the "short" side of the field on long-yardage situations, and have a preference for stunting players to the "wide" side of the field on running situations. If a team does any slanting or looping, it may be detected that it favors slanting or looping to the wide side of the field. A team has been noted to slant only when the ball was on the hash mark, and then only to the wide side of the field.

Another form that can be used is shown in Fig. 7–7. Each defense is

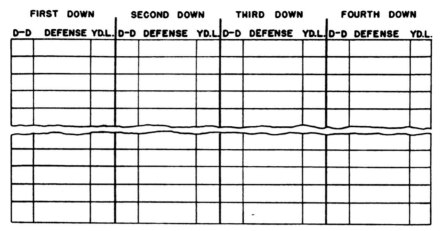

FIRST DOWN			SECOND DOWN			THIRD DOWN			FOURTH DOWN		
D-D	DEFENSE	YD.L.	D-D	DEFENSE	YD.L.	D-D	DEFENSE	YD.L.	D-D	DEFENSE	YD.L.

Fig. 7–7. Defensive down and distance summary sheet.

listed according to down. As you work from the play-by-play, the distance and the position on the field are also recorded. The organization of the information is different from that of the form shown in Fig. 7–6, but again the form would show what defenses are favored in the different down-and-yardage situations, and on what yard line these defenses are employed. Often a team will use a different defense on a third-and-eight situation on the +10 yard line from the one used in the same situation with the ball on the −10 yard line. You can tell where on the field a team will use its short-yardage defense. It is not unusual for a team to refrain from using a short-yardage defense until it reaches a predetermined spot on the field. Other teams may use a short-yardage defense such as a 7–1 defense until the opponent reaches the 50 yard line, and then use an 8–3 inside the 50 yard line. You can determine where on the field a team will start using its goal-line defense.

You should also take note whether, once a defensive team starts using its goal-line defense, it will stay in that defense for the remaining downs of the series. Often if a defensive team is successful in repelling an opponent until the fourth down, it will get into another defense when there are about five or more yards to go for a touchdown. The trend of a defensive team's thinking can be brought out by careful analysis. It can generally be ascertained which defense a defensive team feels is its best defense against running, as well as which one is most effective against the anticipated pass. This knowledge, when obtained, can be used in formulating game plans. You will want to counteract that pattern established for the opponent with whatever weapons are felt to be the most likely to succeed. It may be, for example, that you will want to pass in what is considered the obvious running situation, and to run in what is considered the likeliest passing situation. The defensive team's thinking may make throwing screen passes on a long-yardage situation unattractive to you; it might be best to use this weapon under short-yardage circumstances or on first and ten.

The information recorded in Figs. 7–6 or 7–7 can be used and further

	DEF.	DEF.	DEF.	DEF.	DEF.	DEF.	DEF.	DEF.
1–10								
TOTAL								

LONG YARDAGE

1–L								
2–L								
3–L								
4–L								
TOTAL								

SHORT YARDAGE

2–S								
3–S								
4–S								
TOTAL								

MEDIUM YARDAGE

2-4-5-6								
3-3-4-5								
TOTAL								

Fig. 7–8. Defensive down and distance analysis sheet.

condensed and analyzed under the situations shown in Fig. 7–8. In each of the categories listed, the defenses are recorded along with the total times used. It will become apparent which defenses are favored in each of the situations listed. Not all scouts will need to use all of the forms shown. You should choose those defensive analysis forms which will most easily and quickly show the tendencies your head coach is interested in.

By indicating each defense used in the approximate position on the field, as shown in Fig. 7–9, you can give a more graphic illustration of the defenses, and lines of demarcation can be determined. The brackets on the left side of the chart show how the defenses would be grouped if the field were divided into five equal zones. It seems easier, however, to follow the zoning established by the defenses used, as shown by the brackets on the right side of the chart.

Thus you could instruct your quarterback that from the goal line to the −20 yard line, he will probably be confronted with a Wide 6 and a 7–1 defense. From the −20 yard line to the 50 yard line, another defense may be added, a 6–1. The next zone would be from the 50 to inside the +10 yard line. A 5–3 would be added to the list of probable defenses in this zone. Inside the +10 yard line, the 8–3 could be expected as the goal-line defense, but a 5–3 might also be used. (A check of the down and distance situation as to when each defense was used in each particular zone would give the quarterback a clear picture of what he might expect in each of the zones.) This method of bracketing defenses appears to have more merit than that of arbitrarily setting the zones, since such zoning could present a more complicated picture which would be more difficult to convey to the quarterback.

When the conclusions that can be drawn from the defensive analysis are reached, they can be condensed to the point where they can be listed in brief form. These tendencies will be used in formulating the game plans. The coaches will then have the responsibility of getting the defensive information to the players so that the players know, understand and can use it. If this is not accomplished, the value of scouting is very limited.

Coaches have different approaches that they use in conveying information on which they base their strategy to the players. Such information can be shown on cards and posted in the locker room for study. It can also be given to the quarterbacks to learn. Meetings can be held with the quarterbacks in order that the information can be explained and discussed so that it can be understood. It is imperative that the quarterbacks are able to absorb the material presented to them, so every effort should be made to be organized, concise, and thorough in the presentation of such material. The quarterbacks should know the game plans, and time during practice should be devoted to the quarterbacks' learning these plans.

The quarterbacks and the team can have an opportunity to learn the game plans through practice time devoted to work against the anticipated

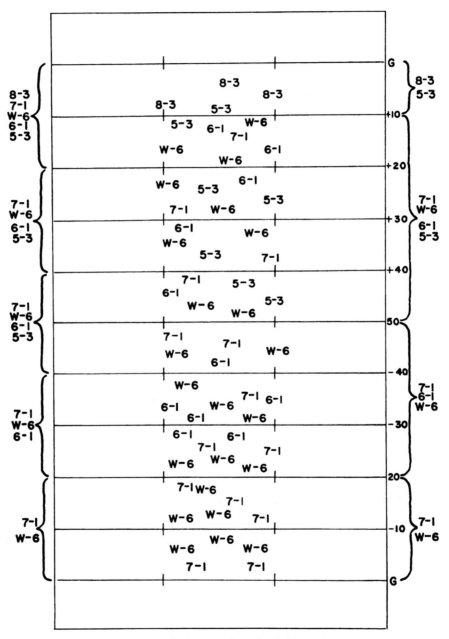

Fig. 7–9. Defensive chart by field position.

defenses. The quarterbacks will naturally run only those plays that are part of the plan for that week. The players will get an opportunity to work against individuals depicting the alignment and play of the opponents. There will be line assignments where the linemen will be able to review assignments of old and new plays. Backs will work to polish those plays that will be used. Time will be spent on pass offense against the anticipated pass defense. Individual work will be given to prepare the players to better handle their opponents. If the opponent employs a middle guard that plays off the ball and is quite active, it is important that your centers work against someone playing in that same manner, if success is to be expected. If the opponent is effective in rushing the passer, it is urgent that time be spent working on pass protection. Whenever possible, either as individuals, by groups, or by teams, opportunities should be provided the players to work against individuals, groups, or teams closely depicting those which will confront them in the game.

Late in the week, the players should be ready to put their knowledge to test under conditions approaching those of a game. One of the best ways to test them is through the use of a "situation" period on the practice field. In this way the coaches can check whether the material presented through the defensive analysis has been absorbed by the team.

In the "situation" period, a freshman, junior varsity, "B" team, or other members of the squad can be used to employ the defenses of the opponent. The same players should be used in this period that during the regular practice sessions were utilized to depict the opponents, and are thus familiar with all that the opponents do. A list of the situations can be given the defensive signal caller, who is to call the defense that would be expected against each situation called. The ball is placed at one end of the field, and the varsity works its way toward its own goal line by running dummy plays against the anticipated defense in the particular situation called (by the coach) at that particular position on the field. For example, the ball might be placed on the —5 yard line. The coach calls out the situation as "first and ten." The defensive team gets into the defense the offensive team should anticipate at that point of the field on first and 10. The defensive team should use the opponent's adjustments from that defense, should any flanker deployment be shown. The offensive team goes into the huddle, the quarterback calls the play, brings the team out of the huddle and runs the play. A manager moves the ball down the field about 5 yards on each play, and varies the field position from hash mark to hash mark. On each down the coach calls out another situation, such as "second and two," not necessarily to coincide with the distance that the manager moved the ball. The quarterback keeps moving the team down the field by putting into use the offensive plans formulated by the coaching staff to be used against the defenses anticipated. This method is exceptionally beneficial in that it gives the coach an opportunity to closely observe the quarterback to see if he has learned the information provided him, and at the same time it gives the quarterback realistic situations that provide him with the opportunity of a "dry run." The offensive line coach also works with the team to see that blocking assignments are properly carried out.

If the coach desires to review phases of the kicking game, he can call a situation that will prompt the signal caller to call for a punt. Emphasis to run plays hurriedly is stressed in order to give the team, and especially the quarterback, a simulated game situation. The team can move down the field until a "touchdown" is scored. Then, if desired, a little more time can be spent on goal-line plays, and after scoring, two point plays, if that is part of the strategy.

After the first "dry run" for a "touchdown," additional situations can be added to those of the down, yardage, and position on the field, by calling out a score and time to play. The coach might say, "We are leading 14–8 with four minutes to play. It is first and ten on the —45 yard line." This gives the quarterback the chance to put into use the strategy set up by the coaching staff to control the ball. It also impresses the team with the importance of learning to play deliberate football, to not go out of bounds, call time out, or do anything to stop the clock.

After this situation has been practiced, the coach might put the ball on the +40 yard line and say, "The score is 16–14 against us with two minutes to play. We have two time outs remaining." Now the quarterback and the team must think in terms of speeding up play, stopping the clock by running out of bounds, and throwing possession or sideline passes where the receiver can get out of bounds after gaining as much yardage as possible. If the opponent has shown a Prevent defense, the defensive team would employ it to give the quarterback, and the team, the opportunity to practice strategy in attacking it. It must be stressed that in this situation stopping the clock is of the utmost importance. No unnecessary chances should be taken in this respect. If a place kicker of some ability is a member of the squad, thought must be given to getting him and the holder into the game, if necessary. If the place kicker is already on the team, then it is important that the kicking tee be obtained without sustaining a penalty. A half-hour on situations can be quite profitable to a football team in getting the thinking and planning of the coaching staff across to the team in general, and to the quarterback in particular. It hardly seems adequate to have a quarterback memorize or carry out offensive planning on the blackboard, and not give him the benefit of planned practice time under conditions as close as possible to those anticipated in the game.

An additional few minutes at the end of practice several nights a week devoted to running the scoring or goal-line plays against the anticipated goal-line defense can also be time spent profitably. This might be done live once or twice, but even if it is done dummy, it can be of tremendous value.

Only by making such preparations against individuals as well as team patterns can the material from the defensive analysis be fully utilized and the opportunity for success made greater. This preparation will be accomplished by working with individuals, groups, and teams, to insure the full understanding of the game plans and the reasons behind them. If great care is taken to fully prepare everyone, and especially the quarterback, then the team will have the confidence necessary to carry out its duties successfully.

8

Scouting the Offense

The general instructions for pregame observation of the defense, as discussed in Chapter 6 (the arrival at the game, the pregame warm-up, etc.), will, of course, apply likewise to scouting the offense. Those instructions will not be repeated in this chapter, but the author would like to again emphasize the importance of the scout's being alert throughout the warm-up for any information that could be helpful to his team.

Most scouts like to treat the kicking game as a separate phase of football. This should be true as regards working with the final report, but at the game it appears easier and less confusing to think of kickoff returns, punts, and quick kicks as part of the offensive phase of football, and will be considered thus in this chapter.

RECEIVING THE KICKOFF

In noting the deployment of the various players in receiving a kickoff, it is generally a good idea to start with the backs and work upfield to the linemen. The rules restrict the alignment of the first five men, while the other six players have some freedom as to where they can be deployed. The number of each back and where he is lined up should be noted, as it might be that one player is especially dangerous as a kickoff returner, and thus you may decide to keep the kick away from him. His exact depth is of little consequence, since this is dictated by the kicker and possibly the wind conditions. Some head coaches want the exact alignment and the numbers of all players on the receiving team, and therefore this should be obtained. The use of binoculars is highly recommended to get the numbers of all the players.

Once the receiving team is set for the kickoff, and as the ball is kicked (do not watch the kicker), maximum concentration should be directed to the five front men to see what they do. They are going to make their moves before the ends and the backs, since the latter must wait to see where the ball is going before they can initiate their action. These five front men, by their actions, will often quickly indicate what the direction of the return will be. If they all start back and go to one side, or if one or two wait until the kicking team comes downfield so they can peel off behind the kicking team, it is obvious that an outside return is taking place. As soon as this is established, the scout should look to the end and back on the side of the return to see who is going to pair up to double team, and on whom. It can usually be determined quickly where the running lane is being established.

If the five front men drop straight back, look to see if there is any cross blocking on either side of the center man. If the center man goes right out for the kicker, quickly focus your attention on the other four men to see what they are going to do. As soon as you see them start their moves, look to the ends and backs to see how they are coordinated with the linemen.

Should the five front men drop straight back to form a wedge, immediately focus your attention on the ends and backs to see how they work themselves into the wedge. In watching a kickoff return develop, the scout will find it much easier to think of the return as two distinct actions—one by the front line and the other by the backs and ends. Since the front-line action begins first, concentrate on the front men to see what action they are starting, and as you see the return form, focus your attention on the rest of the team to see the second action. The first group will start as soon as the ball is kicked while the second group will generally wait until the first has started to get into position before the second starts to run at full speed. Nothing of any value as far as the return is concerned can be obtained by watching the kicker kick the ball, and then following the ball in flight down the field.

Notations should be made on the type of returns used and the effectiveness. Often it will be difficult to get a clear picture of who is involved in the key blocks on the return as a result of a very short kick or one that was kicked on the ground. However, a general picture of the type of return utilized should be obtained, and can be if the proper observations are made in their logical sequence. Should one particular back be especially effective in returning kicks, this should be noted and emphasized in the report in order that the kicker can be instructed not to kick the ball to that player. Any returns of a tricky nature should also be emphasized. Often one player may stand out as being exceptionally slow or a fumbler, and this information could lead to plans for kicking the ball to such a player, if at all possible.

OFFENSIVE PLAY BY PLAY

It is important that you get complete and accurate information when charting the offensive play by play, because from this play-by-play tendencies can be obtained that can be helpful in formulating game plans. (These tendencies will be covered in a later chapter.)

Before a team starts an offensive series, make a note as to how the team gained possession of the football. Indicate whether the team recovered a fumble, intercepted a pass, blocked a kick, received a kick, or held the other team on downs. One reason for this information is that some coaches feel it is often very profitable to throw a long pass after getting the ball from a team as a result of a so-called "break" such as an interception, fumble, or blocked kick. The feeling is that the team or possibly the player involved in the play might be feeling sorry for himself and will be still thinking about the mistake to the extent that he will not be concentrating on defense, and thus be vulnerable to a long pass. In scouting the fine Tennessee teams under the tutelage of General Robert R. Neyland, the author was amazed at how many times Tennessee would throw a pass after getting the ball on a so-called "break," and also how many times this proved successful in getting a long gain or a touchdown. Naturally, Tennessee did not try it every time, even though the field position was favorable, but did it often enough to make you feel that it was part of the offensive thinking, and that you should caution your deep defenders to be especially alert.

While the team is in the huddle, mark the play-by-play chart in the appropriate square as to the down, yardage, hash mark and yard line. If the ball is anywhere between the hash marks, even a yard inside one of them, it would seem best to indicate that as middle of the field, and consider all such placements in that category. There must be a line of distinction, and the hash mark itself appears to be the clearest place to make that distinction. If this is not done, and those balls 1 yard inside the hash mark are marked Left, what is the classification to be if the ball is 2 yards inside the hash mark? However, it should be added that some head coaches will instruct that anything within 5 yards of the hash mark is to be considered on that hash mark and so indicated, and everything within the two imaginary lines to be considered the middle of the field. Naturally, the scout's line of distinction will be that desired by the head coach.

As the team comes out of the huddle, look for any backs that are going out as flankers and for any ends that might be splitting wide. If you are using some code, abbreviations, or a brief system of calling formations, you can indicate the formation without taking your eyes off the playing field. This can be done in the same way as in the defensive play by play—by having your pencil set and poised on the paper in the appropriate space, and as you see the formation, simply indicate it. Then, for example, if the left halfback is going out as a flanker to the left, you can mark that as A-1. At the conclusion of the play, if the flanker was directly involved in the play, you might want to cross out the circle on the worksheet representing his normal alignment and draw another circle indicating his flanker position and his new assignment on the play. Some scouts look at the formation, watch the play, and then do whatever writing and drawing is necessary to adequately show the formation and the play. If the play is the same as one in your offense, it is very simple to write that number above the formation. However, any differences in the scouted team's execution of the play from the way your team runs it should be carefully noted. Regardless of the method of recording that you use, it is important that your method allow you to see and properly record the formation, backfield action, and the hole through which the play was run. You must be systematic, quick, and concise in your recording.

Early in the game it should be noted whether the team comes out of the huddle and the players get down in their stance as soon as they reach the line of scrimmage, or if they line up with their hands or elbows on their knees, and then go to a set position on the command of the quarterback. If they come out in an up position, be alert to see if they ever run plays from that position, especially in short-yardage situations.

It should also be noted how long the offensive team is at the line of scrimmage before the start of the play. This does not mean you must keep track of the time with a stop watch, but rather visualize yourself on defense and determine whether you would have time to change defenses, if you so desired. It can generally be ascertained, also, if the quarterback has the option to check off to a new play at the line of scrimmage by the way he approaches the ball and his actions after he places his hands in position to receive the snap. If he is deliberate and looks the defense over thoroughly, chances are that he can change plays at the line. You might also watch to see whether he looks straight ahead when he approaches the line. If he comes up to the line hurriedly, with his head and eyes straight ahead, in all probability the plays will be run as called in the huddle. These are impressions that should be either remembered or written down when time permits, but should be expressed as opinions. The only sure way to find out if the quarterback is checking off, and also to get his cadence at the line of scrimmage, is to have some one go down to the side line and listen. This can be done easily if you are working with another scout. Another possibility is to talk with the players of the opposing team after the game. This is not as good a method as it would seem, however, since there are often as many different opinions as the number of players questioned.

In order to improve in scouting, every time the team comes up to the line of scrimmage one should try to condition himself to get or to check at least one thing more than the basic information—the formation, play action, and the hole through which the play was run. The speed with which the plays are run will determine how many extra points you can observe. Regardless of how fast the plays are run, a scout should note the line splits of at least two linemen on a play. A definite pattern should be developed that can be followed every time in checking the line splits. This can be done by working the line from the inside out or from the outside in. Regardless of which method is used, eventually the entire line should be observed and the splits between the players involved noted on the worksheets.

Since the splits of the guards and tackles are usually limited, it seems simpler to record them in feet, while the splits involving the ends are generally wider and can be recorded in yards. Thus, the figure 1 between the center and guard or between the guard and tackle would indicate a split of 1 foot, while the figure 1 between the tackle and end would indicate a split of 1 yard.

The splits of ends should be given close scrutiny as they often provide the best play tip-offs. It is not unusual for an end to split a little wider than normal on a pass play in order to better enable him to get into his pattern without being delayed by a defensive player. Some ends will split wider on plays away from them, and others might do it to get a more advantageous position to hook the defensive end on plays to his side. In order to get any play tip-offs, a scout must condition himself to look for them.

Once the basic line splits are established, periodically they should be re-checked to see if there is any change, and thus any tip-off. Some teams will cut down on their splits on pass plays in order to make the protection easier for the linemen. They might also cut them down on wide plays to enable the ball carrier to have less distance to run to get around the end and to the outside. Wide line splits are often used to try to entice the defensive men to split with them, and thus make it more inviting to run inside plays.

Generally, the line splits of a team now do not vary as much as they did when the Split T was in such wide use, but it is still important to check them for any tip-offs. Even though no tip-offs may be forthcoming, the defensive line coach, or whoever is responsible for setting the line defenses, should want to know what basic line splits will be confronted.

Once the basic line splits are established, the scout can concentrate on other things that may prove of value. If the team is deliberate at the line of scrimmage, much more should be checked. Possibly of more importance than line splits is the alignment and position of the backfield men. With close observation one can often detect great variance in where they line up in relation to each other as well as their depth from the line of scrimmage. More often than not, they will take positions that will enable them to carry out their assignments with the greatest dispatch possible. It is very seldom that a halfback will line up in the same relative position when he is to block the defensive end out, as he will when he must block him in. The halfback will usually line up closer to the line of scrimmage and not too wide when he is assigned to block the end out, while he will get wider and deeper if he is supposed to block him in. It is much easier to detect a variance in alignment in the normal T formation with no flankers, but the variance can still be noted if there is one back being flanked. Wingbacks will also vary their positions a great deal, depending upon their assignments.

Whether it be by chance or design, the alignment of the offensive line in relationship to the football can vary a great deal, and this would be of great importance to some defensive line coaches. Some offensive lines will take their position on the line from the football, while other teams will have their line take their position from some part of the center. For example, in the former case when the guards come up to the line of scrimmage, they will line up as close to the tip of the football as possible. The tackles take their position from the guards, and the ends take theirs from the tackles. This puts the whole line up on the football. Other teams will have their offensive line back of the football, and they will take their position in a different manner. The guard may line up with his toes even or slightly behind the heel of the center's forward foot. The tackles and ends then line up with their hand even with the hand of the guard on their side of the line. This method puts the center out in front of the rest of the linemen by some 12–15 inches. The two lines, with the exceptions of the centers, could vary their positions considerably in relationship to the football.

When the defensive line takes its position from the football, there could be a difference of some 12–15 inches between the offensive and defensive linemen, depending on where the offensive team lined up. This difference in distance could affect the play of the defensive players, since it could cause them to overextend themselves to make contact with the offensive lineman opposite them, or it could result in their having to take an extra step that they are not used to taking.

When the defensive line takes its alignment from the offensive players, the relative distance between the offensive and defensive lines will be the same regardless of where the offensive line lines up. However, since the defensive team would probably prefer to take its position from the football, many defensive coaches want to know whether the offensive line is up on the ball or if the players are back of the ball any noticeable distance. This knowledge should be of importance to a team that does considerable stunting, since it can affect the success or failure of this type of defense. It takes longer for a stunt to materialize, and thus would give the offensive team more time to adjust to a stunt, if the offensive line is back of the ball rather than lined up right on it. There is no problem as far as the middle guard is concerned on an odd defense, provided he is playing over the offensive center, but on an even defense all linemen would be affected.

There have been instances in which the defensive line has played off the ball nearly 3 feet against teams that were lined up back of the ball approximately fifteen inches, and with great success. The offensive line had never been faced with this picture before and had difficulty in getting and maintaining blocks. This type of defensive play, however, would not be recommended against all types of offense.

Once the various checks have been made of the offensive alignment of the questions that will be asked of the scout, all concentration should be directed to the start and development of the offensive play. There are a variety of patterns that can and should be used in watching the play unfold. One pattern that can be used is to focus on the triangle formed by the two guards and the fullback (assuming that he is in his normal position). As the quarterback receives the ball and starts his action, observe the action within that triangle. Watch the two guards start their action and make a mental note of what they did. At the completion of the play, record it, along with the backfield action and anything else of importance that was noted in the development of the play. It should be remembered that in order for the quarterback to get the ball to any back on a direct hand-off, either the quarterback or the receiving back will have to take at least two steps, or there will be a total of at least that number of steps to execute the hand-off. This will give you an opportunity to observe the interior linemen start their action, and then switch your attention to the backfield. Care should be taken to avoid getting so engrossed in the line play as to miss the movements of the backs.

Another pattern that can be used in order to observe a different area of play is to watch the backfield action begin, and as soon as you can determine the flow of the play, immediately concentrate your attention on the end and tackle to the side that the play is going. For example, if the quarterback is handing the ball to the left halfback going to the right, look to the right end and tackle to see what their assignments are. You can usually tell quickly if there is a double team block, or if one of those two players is going through for a linebacker, or if the end is trying to hook the defensive end. If there is a wingback on that side, concentrate on the wingback and end to see what they do. At other times, in a T formation with no flankers, look to the right halfback and fullback as soon as you have established that the flow of the play is to the right.

If a team uses flankers wider than a wingback (1 yard outside of the offensive end), the same approach can be used to find out if the flankers are utilized as blockers. As soon as it is determined that the flow is toward the flanker, attention should be focused on the flanker to see what he does, and then work back toward the ball carrier. If the flanker goes downfield to block, or blocks a defensive man to his inside, immediately look back to the ball carrier to see who is leading the play. This same method can be used in checking a split end to see what he does on various plays.

When a play starts with a pitch out by the quarterback, either a deep pitch to the fullback, or a wide pitch to the halfback, look to the widest offensive man in the direction of the play, as he is generally the key blocker.

By changing your pattern in looking at a play develop, you make different observations which you can put together after the game and can have a fairly complete picture of how the team blocks its favorite plays. Naturally, if a team does not run a certain play too many times, you might not get as complete a picture of that play as you would like, but you would have the backfield action and some of the blocking at the point of attack.

Regardless of what pattern or patterns are being used in observing a play develop, very little time should be spent in watching the ball exchange between the quarterback and the ball carrier. There are other and more important things happening before this takes place, and these should be observed. A common tendency is to watch the exchange and then the ball carrier run with the ball. When this is done, however, about the only impressions that are obtained are how well the other team exchanges the ball and how well the ball carriers can run. It is important to vary the patterns of watching plays develop in order to get a more complete picture of the offense. At times you must watch the line to get the blocking as well as any tip-offs by the linemen on play action passes. Many times the backs will fake superbly, but the linemen will set up to pass protect, and thus give the defense the tip-off necessary to stop the play.

It should also be remembered that although the play is over and the whistle has blown, the search for information should not cease. The scout can check the area of the defensive backs, for example, to see who has gone downfield to block. He might check to see where the quarterback is to determine his action after handing off the ball to another back. Very often similar important bits of knowledge can be gotten after the play has ended.

In scouting a team that passes with some regularity, a scout can obtain much information throughout the course of one ball game. If two scouts are working together, the responsibilities can be divided, and consequently more information obtained. Even when working alone, a scout's attention can be directed to some phase of the pass offense for a quick check to get something specific on each pass, and then look to get the pass pattern.

As in scouting the running offense, a scout can have several different patterns of scouting that can be followed; these fall right in line with the techniques he would use in observing the running offense. If you are watching the triangle of the fullback and the two guards, by the action of any—and possibly all three—of these players you can determine quickly if a drop back pass is developing. On the snap of the ball, both guards will usually set up for pass protection blocks, and in most cases the fullback will also. The natural inclination, as soon as a pass play shows, is to look downfield to see what receivers are going downfield and what patterns they are running. However, much information can be obtained before you should look downfield. It takes a matter of several seconds for the pattern to develop, so while it is developing, checks should be made on some other phases of the play, or players, to get the answers to some of the questions that will undoubtedly be asked of the scout.

In watching the quarterback, the scout can follow him as he fades back to pass so that the scout can get information on the quarterback's actions. The speed with which he goes back and his depth can be of importance. Of possibly much greater importance is to find out if the passer is looking at a specific area or receiver as he fades back, thus indicating where he is going to throw the ball before it actually leaves his hand. Many pass defense coaches predicate much of their teaching on watching the passer's eyes and teach the defenders to react or be able to react in that direction, and thus get a "jump" on the ball. This knowledge can make the difference between a defender's being at the right spot and preventing a completion, or not being there and having the pass be completed. There are indeed very few passers in college or high school football who can adequately conceal their intentions in this respect.

The scout should also note whether the passer "back pedals," or if he runs back sideways, or if he turns his back and runs back to set up to pass. His depth and speed should have a bearing on the method employed to rush him, or it may determine whether rushes or coverage will be emphasized. If the passer turns his back in going back to pass, it may be that you will want to shoot a linebacker from a blind side a great deal of the time. All these bits of information can be of value in setting up defenses against your opponent.

If a quarterback uses several methods to go back to pass, he will usually have a reason for it. On some types of passes, he will go back one way, and on passes to a certain area he may use a different technique. As proficient as most professional quarterbacks are, there are several in the National Football League that generally tip-off the area to which they are going to pass, or the area where their primary receiver is. When they "back pedal," they are usually going to throw the ball to the left, and when they run back sideways, they generally throw the ball over the middle or to the right. Since two of these passers are high in the list of those passers with the most interceptions, it seems that some of their opponents are aware of this tip-off. This is not to be interpreted to mean that as soon as a quarterback "backpedals," all of the defenders should immediately run to the left, since the passer will, if his protection holds up, look to another area or receiver if his primary target is covered. It can, however, affect those defenders who, as a result of the pattern or the defense, have no immediate responsibility and thus can favor that side of the field. This knowledge could be especially valuable, for example, to the play of linebackers. Since the passer is the man with the football, it is important to get as much knowledge about him as can be obtained. Most of the passers will tell you not only where they are going to throw the ball before they actually let loose of it, but their action in going back to pass can also be helpful in determining the type of pass defense adjustments that might be used.

Since the passer must go back and set up before throwing the football, the scout can observe his actions and still get the pass pattern. The individual maneuvers of the receivers will go unobserved while the scout is watching the quarterback, but the receivers' position and the direction they are going can be seen. There is still a period of time that elapses between the moment when the passer actually sets up to throw the ball and when the ball actually leaves his hand. This is when the scout should look to the receivers. It must be remembered that when sufficient knowledge is obtained about the passer, the scout can then concentrate on the receivers when he first recognizes that a pass play is coming.

Another important bit of information can be gotten by watching the passer and then looking downfield to get the pass pattern. If the passer is looking to an area or to a particular receiver as he fades back to pass, look away from that area to see if there are any receivers going downfield, and note if they are running their pass route with the same effort that the primary receiver is running his. Often in college and high school football, the primary receiver will run his route full speed, and the so-called decoys simply go through the motions of running their pass routes. Even if the ball is thrown while you are watching the receivers, and the pass is incomplete, look to the area where the ball was thrown and check who the possible receivers were and their positions. Draw the pass pattern and indicate the intended receiver and his number. At the conclusion of the game, you will want to see how many passes were thrown to each of the receivers so you can indicate which ones can be considered the favorites. The action of the quarterback, whether it be drop back, play action, or roll out, should be indicated along with the pass pattern. If the pass was completed, the gain should, of course, be shown.

If the quarterback is rushed, and has to run with the football, still consider the play as a pass in your own analysis of the game, although the official game statistics will consider it as a run. Indicate the yardage gained or lost along with the notation Rushed or Ran. This way you can get a very good idea of the effectiveness of the passer as a runner, as well as of the team's pass protection. If the pass protection breaks down often, in making defensive game plans it should certainly be considered to emphasize rushing the passer rather than coverage.

Many quarterbacks will telegraph their intentions for a screen pass in the way that they set up. Whereas a passer will ordinarily go back 5 to 7 yards to pass, many passers will run back as fast as possible to depths of as much as 10 or 12 yards when they are going to throw a screen pass. If this is the case with the quarterback you are watching, such information should be made a part of your notes.

If the scout is using the pattern of observing offensive plays develop by watching the flow of the play and then looking to the side of the line that the play is going to, and a pass play develops, you might quickly check the backs' pass protection before you look for the pass pattern. If you should want to concentrate on the pattern, another method of observation can be helpful, and that is to consciously widen your field of vision to cover a wide area. Think in terms of watching an area covering the space between the defensive backs. By doing this, you can see three or four receivers, but do not expect to see every move that they make. You can get a general picture of where they go and how deep they are. To do this, however, you must be sitting high in the stands and must condition yourself to look at a wide area.

An important point to remember, whether you are scouting for the first time or have a great deal of experience, is to change your pattern of looking at plays develop in order to see more and different phases of the play. If you use the same pattern every time, you are going to be seeing the same things every time, and this is not conducive to getting a total scouting report.

SCOUTING THE KICKING GAME

In this phase of scouting there is a great deal of difference in methods used by scouts, and is the part of the report least studied by many coaches. The emphasis on this part of the game will vary considerably. Some scouts go to a game equipped with stop watches to time the punters in pregame and actual game kicking, while others are concerned only with the basic punt formation, the punters, and some general notes on the kicking game. Of course, any coach should want to know about the obviously slow punter, but there are many who do not analyze the scouting report on the kicking game with the same thoroughness with which they approach the analysis of the offense and defense.

One of the first things that should be checked is the basic punt formation used, in terms of alignment, splits, and depth of kicker. The first time that a team kicks, the formation can be observed and noted, along with a check of the kicker as to the number of steps that he takes, the distance of his kick, and the type of kick. While observing this, it is a simple matter to also see how well the center gets the ball back to the kicker. You can get a general idea of his effectiveness from the pregame observation, but it is often a different matter when he must do it under pressure. Usually teams are deliberate in lining up into punt formation, so you might check to see if the defensive team has a man head up to the center. This could affect the center's success in getting the ball back to the punter.

If the distance of the kick is important to you, an easy way to estimate the approximate distance is to make a mental note of how far the safety men or safety man is from the line of scrimmage. Then, as the ball is kicked, watch and see how far the receiver has to come up or go back to catch the ball. If the safetymen are lined up 30 yards from the ball, for instance, it is an easy matter to watch them and see how much of an adjustment the receiver has to make to catch the ball.

An important item to note the succeeding time you watch the team punt is how well the team covers kicks. As the ball is snapped, look to the linemen to see how fast they release, and follow their movement downfield. As one or more men move out in front of the rest of the team, determine who they are and how far they are from the receiver when he catches the ball. See if there is a big area between the front men and the rest of the team, or if there are many of the players close behind. If a team covers kicks very effectively, then it might be best to suggest that punt rushes be used every time, in hopes that a punt might be blocked, or that under heavy pressure the kicker would not get off good kicks.

By nature of the type of play that a punt is, there is usually plenty of time to check a variety of things. The team is generally deliberate in lining up, the ball has to be passed quite a distance, the punter takes some time to kick the ball, and the height and distance of the kick also take time. A scout can observe many phases of the kicking game on each punt used in the game.

A special notation should be made if anything other than a kick is used from punt formation. If the team has shown any history of this in the past, it should be so stated in the final report, so that adequate precautions can be taken.

If the team uses the quick kick at any time, this should also be shown in the report, and the knowledge used at the discretion of the coach. The player that does the kicking as well as the method of getting the ball to him should be shown. Some teams will have the quarterback pitch the ball back to the quick kicker, while others will get the ball to the kicker by a direct snap from center. If a direct snap is used, the offensive center will have to put his head down in order to see the back that he is snapping the ball to, and this should be called to the attention of the defensive linemen playing over or near the offensive center.

Since the Rules Committee has authorized the widening of the goal posts, there has been a much more prevalent use of the field goal as an offensive weapon. When the team tries a field goal, a notation should be made of both the holder and the kicker, and their depth. If the holder is a quarterback, the defensive backs should be cautioned against a fake field goal attempt, and alerted to a pass. The scout should observe at least one side of the line to determine the players' effectiveness as protectors, and hope that another opportunity will be available later in the game so that he can watch the other side—on either another field goal attempt or on a point after touchdown. If, however, the first (and perhaps only) opportunity occurs late in the game, then you must watch the whole line as best you can, in order to see if an area appears weak in its protection.

Another new rule that has affected the game considerably in college ball, and in high schools as well, is the option of the team scoring the touchdown to kick for one point, or to run or pass for two points. This phase of the game should be given the same close scrutiny as all others.

The place kick formation should be viewed for any weaknesses which might enable your team to block a kick. Since most place kicks are blocked as a result of penetration from the inside, this should be an area that would come under especially close attention. It is seldom that place kicks are blocked from the outside, but it does happen if extremely fast men are used to rush from the outside. The depth of the kicker is important, too. If the holder is more than 8 yards from the ball, and most teams will get 7, he is inviting trouble. Speedy rushers from the outside can get in deep enough to get in line with the flight of the ball. When the team being scouted is to be seen several times, each side of the line should be given individual examination for any weaknesses. Often a football team will have one player who is considerably lighter than the rest of his teammates on the line. When this is the case, he should be observed closely; it could be that this player can be overpowered, and thus would enable your team to force an opening that could lead to the blocking of the kick.

If utilized, the two-point play after a touchdown should be scouted the same as any other play in any offensive series. It should, however, be noted whether the team depends on the same type plays that led to the touchdown for its two-point attempt, or whether the team goes to something tricky or different. Some coaches feel that if their team is successful in taking the ball downfield for a touchdown on running plays, it should continue with the same type attack in the two-point situation. With some teams the plays used for the two-point attempt are those that fall into their short-yardage category, and when this is true, it should be duly noted.

Since the score of the game will in many cases dictate whether the team is going to go for one or two points, it is important to note the score of the game at the time of the PAT or two-point attempt. When the score and time remaining practically compel a team to make the only logical choice, this choice should not be considered as the selection that would necessarily by made under different conditions.

In scouting for your particular team, you may find that you need to include other observations in addition to those mentioned here, or even to omit some which have been suggested in order to appropriately allot your time. This is the great value of a check-list: a scout then knows exactly which points he should spend his time on. It is imperative that he get the information which is vital to the success of his team.

9

Offensive Analysis

As soon as possible after the completion of the ball game, the scout should begin compiling his report, which will, of course, include the offensive analysis. Many different analyses can be made to try to uncover tendencies that will be helpful in preparing game plans. Some of these analyses will be discussed in this chapter. Regardless of the types of analyses the scout may choose, his material should be organized in some logical manner. The organization preferred by the author is as follows: analysis of (1) play distribution by offensive formations, (2) down and yardage tendencies, (3) running plays, and (4) passing plays.

PLAY DISTRIBUTION FROM OFFENSIVE FORMATIONS

In preparing the formation and play distribution chart, a scout can follow any one of several methods. Regardless of method, the formations should be drawn in the order of importance to the opponent's attack. One method of showing distribution by formation is shown in Fig. 9–1. Each play run from that formation is shown, as well as the success or failure of the play. (There are some coaches who are interested only in the number of times that each hole was attacked, and are not interested in knowing the success of each play.)

The plays should be indicated by numbers which correspond with your numbering system and letters which coincide with abbreviations of your terms describing the different types of blocking. If a different color is used to indicate each different back, you can look at the diagram and tell at a glance where each back likes to run. (It is very simple to use a red pencil for the left halfback plays, a blue for the fullback, and so on.) In Fig. 9–1 you get a complete picture of the offensive plays run from that one formation, and the yardage gained or lost by each play. If desired, a composite of each play can be shown above the hole. For example, you would show that 29J was run three times for a total gain of 12 yards. This can be done with each play, so the information is available for any coach who wants it.

In the lower right-hand corner a brief summary of the passes thrown from

TOTAL PLAYS __22__   PERCENTAGE __46 %__

48J+9	46B+1			21QT+4		27B+2 TD	29S−1
48S+12	46F+2			31W +2		+2	29J+4
+10	+3			31QT+7		27F+8	+1
				+3		+11	+7
				+5		+2	

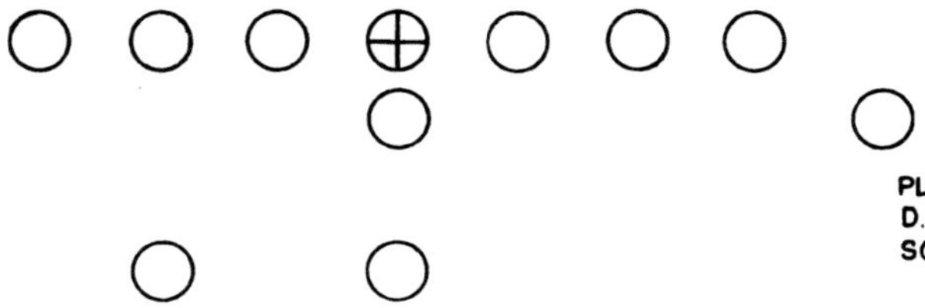

○ ○ ○ ⊕ ○ ○ ○

○   ○

PLAY PASSES - 2
D. B. P.   - 0
SCREENS   - 0

○   ○

RUNS __20__   PASSES __2__

Fig. 9–1. A method of offensive analysis by formation.

the formation is given. There were two play passes. They are listed, along with the gain on each. The letters DBP indicate drop back passes. There were no drop back passes and no screens thrown from this formation. The total number of runs is shown in the lower left-hand corner of the diagram, the total number of plays from this formation is in the upper left-hand corner. The percentage indicated in the remaining corner shows how much this formation was used in relation to the total offensive plays run in the entire game.

Another method of showing play distribution from a formation is shown in Fig. 9–2. A different colored pencil is used to show the course of each back as he carried the ball. Only the left halfback is shown in this illustration, since it is not in color. This method gives you a quick and concise picture of where each back ran, and his success. It is the method preferred by the author. Fig. 9–2 shows the same distribution for the left halfback as is shown in Fig. 9–1. In any method, when colored pencils are used, it is important that the same color be designated for each back every time, and that all scouts adhere to the use of these same colors.

Some scouts will go a step further and will show the distribution from each formation in the three positions of the field—the left hash mark, the middle of the field, and the right hash mark. This type of charting is shown in Fig. 9–3. As you go through the offensive play by play, you record each play by formation in the proper field position. For example, in the first row, all the plays run from the right hash mark from the normal T formation would be shown in the top right square. All the plays run from the middle of the field from the same formation would be shown in the top

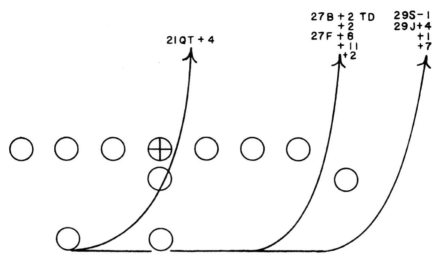

Fig. 9–2. A variation of offensive analysis by formation.

middle square, while those run from the normal T formation from the left hash mark would be shown in the top left square. Each formation used in the game, together with the plays run from it, is charted in the same manner.

The pass offense is shown by tabulating each pass play according to the type of pass it was, the action of the quarterback, the approximate area it was thrown to, and the intended receiver. The abbreviations beneath each formation are: Sc, screen pass; ROP, roll out pass; PP, play pass; and DBP, drop back pass. As the scout goes through the play by play, he records each pass. For example, if from the right hash mark from a normal T formation, the quarterback threw a screen pass to the right, a mark would be made under Sc on the right. The intended receiver would be indicated by the position he played. If the quarterback rolled out to the right, the pass would be indicated under ROP on the right. If a play action pass was used with the faking of the play going to the right, that would be marked under PP on the right. All drop back passes would be shown under DBP. All passes to the left would, of course, be shown on the left under the abbreviation of the proper type of pass.

An analysis of this type can often show much more than a breakdown by formation, or a tabulation of hash mark tendencies disregarding formation. It will show whether a team likes to run into the side line or to the wide side of the field from a certain formation. By merely checking all running plays that were run from the right hash mark, regardless of formation, the distribution will often be fairly even between running into the side line and going to the wide side of the field. In an analysis of the type shown in

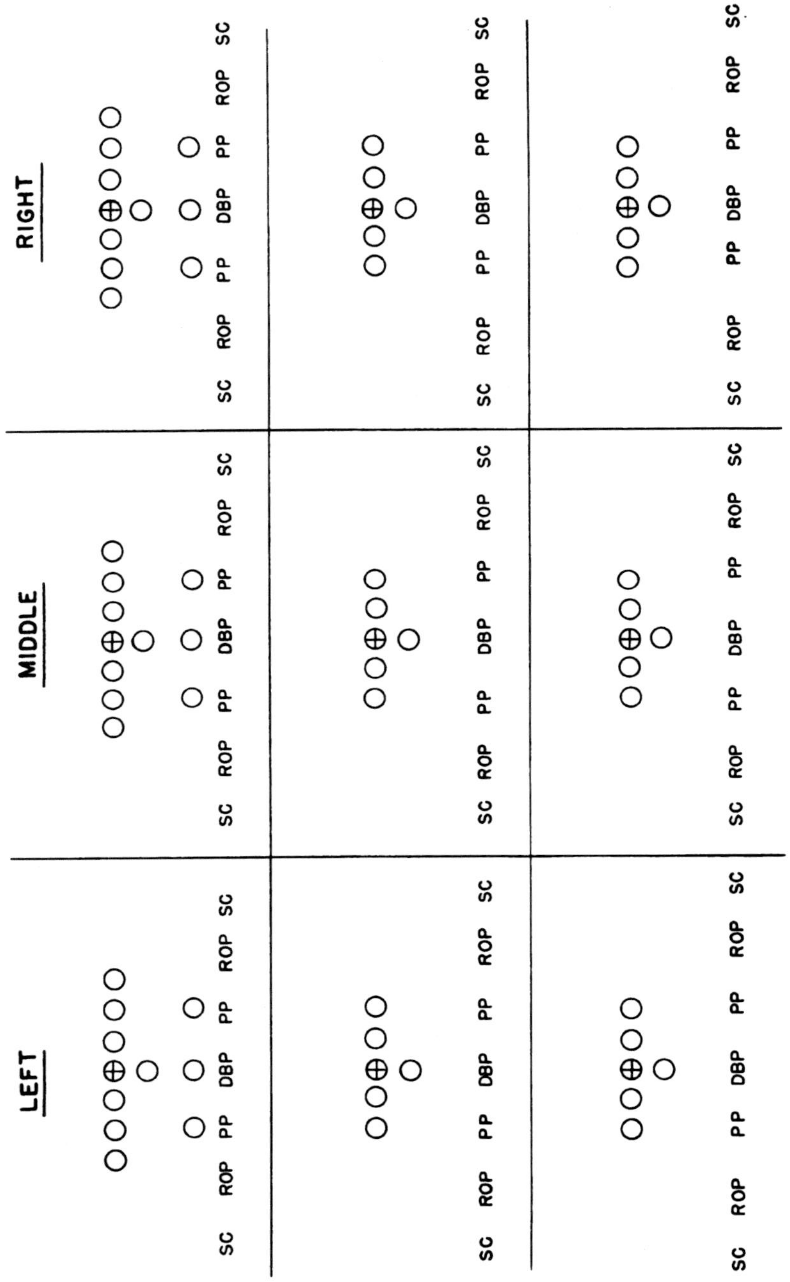

Fig. 9–3. Formation play distribution by field position.

Fig. 9–3, however, it would become apparent if a team favored going into the side line from one formation and favored the wide side of the field from another formation. Charting the distribution of all passes thrown can also produce some interesting tendencies on this form. It is not unusual to find a team that will throw a certain type pass into the side line from a particular formation. Some teams will never throw a play action pass into the side line while others will throw screen passes only into the side line.

It is important to know if a team will favor running to one side from a particular formation but will throw most of its passes to the other side of the field. This can be easily noted if it is properly tabulated. If you look at only the running distribution, the normal reaction would be to adjust the defenses to stop the running. However, an adjustment to stop the running might weaken the defense against passing. If a team is not made aware of an opponent's strength in passing, and the area to which the passes are thrown, an adjustment to stop only the running could bring dire results.

DOWN AND YARDAGE TENDENCIES

The form shown in Fig. 9–4 can be used to show the down and distance, the play that was run, and the gain. Every play in the game is charted. At the end of the form, each hole, together with the total times each hole was attacked on each down, is shown. This can give some indication of where a team likes to run on each down. The passes for each down are also totaled, which can help give some idea as to when a team prefers to pass.

The wavy lines indicate the end of an offensive series. In reading through the chart, you can get some idea of a team's offensive thinking. For example, in looking at the first down situations, you can see that the quarterback likes to repeat successful plays. The first time that 27F was run it resulted in a gain of 15 yards, and the quarterback came right back with the same play. This tendency is shown again when 29J gained 22 yards, and the play was immediately repeated. The form also shows that this team evidently did not believe in passing on first down unless it was a long-yardage situation, and then a screen pass was thrown.

When the team got down near the goal line, it favored running the fullback anywhere from tackle to tackle. These particular plays should be checked to see if the goal-line plays are the same ones preferred on short-yardage situations.

On second down, there is evidence of some definite tendencies. On a short-yardage situation, the quarterback likes to throw a play pass; this is brought to light twice. Once on second and two, he faked to the fullback, and on a second and three situation, he faked to the halfback, and in both instances, threw a play-action pass. (The defensive secondary must be alerted to such a tendency.) Evidence is also shown here that he does like to

FIRST DOWN			SECOND DOWN			THIRD DOWN			FOURTH DOWN		
D-D	PLAY	GN	D-D	PLAY	GN	D-D	PLAY	GN	D-D	PLAY	GN
1-10	29 J	+2	2-8	46 B	-1	3-9	DBP	+12			
1-10	48 J	+8	2-2	PLAY PASS OFF 37	INC	3-2	37	+4			
1-10	27 F	+15									
1-10	27 F	+8	2-2	36	+1	3-1	31 W	+2			
1-10	31 QT	-2	2-12	46 B	PEN -5						
			2-17	48	+1	3-16	DBP	INC	4-16	PUNT	
1-15	29 J	+22									
1-10	29 J	PEN -15									
1-25	FB.SC. LT.	0	2-25	DBP	+13	3-12	FB DRAW	+4	4-8	PUNT	
1-10	30 QT	0		(FUMBLE)							
1-10	46 B	+1	2-9	QUICK KICK							
1-10	27 B	+2	2-8	27 F	-3	3-11	DBP	INC	4-11	DBP	+16
1-10	29 J	+7	2-3	PASS OFF 27	+19						
1-4	37 S	+1	2-3	36 S	+1	3-2	31 W	0	4-2	37 S (TD)	+2
1-10	27 F	0	2-10	DBP-RAN	-8	3-18	FB.SC.RT.	+9	4-9	PUNT	
1-10	22	+1	2-9	31 QT	0	3-9	DBP	+14			

HOLE SUMMARY

9 4			
7 5	1	1	1
3			
1 1	1	3	
0 1			
2 1			
6 1	4		
8 1	1		

RUNS	PASSES	RUNS	PASSES	RUNS	PASSES	RUNS	PASSES
14	1	7	4	4	5	1	1

Fig. 9-4. Offensive summary chart.

run the fullback on a short-yardage situation. As in the goal-line situation, it is an off-tackle play. In the two instances that drop back passes were thrown, it was with long yardage to go for a first down. But it was also indicated that the team will not always pass on the long-yardage situation, as witnessed by the quarterback's call of 46B on second down and 12 yards to go. A quick kick was used once on second down, a fact which may be of importance to some coaches, but of little consequence to others.

The charts of the third and fourth down situations further substantiate some tendencies already brought forth. First, the team continued to run the fullback when confronted with short yardage for a first down, and second, the quarterback did like to pass in the obvious passing situation, but he will also keep you honest with an occasional screen pass or draw play.

Another approach to getting much the same type of information is shown in Fig. 9–5. In this case each running play is charted in the proper column, depending on which hole was attacked. The down and distance is shown, the play, and the gain. At the bottom of the form you can show how many times each hole was attacked on each down. Each pass play of the game is shown on the companion sheet. The down and distance, the type of pass (drop back, play action, roll out, or screen), the receiver, and the gain are charted. This can be studied to get the offensive thinking of the team as to when it likes to use certain passes, what the long- and short-yardage preferences are, and who the favorite receiver might be.

If desired, this type of analysis can be carried to a further breakdown, as shown in Fig. 9–6. Each down is classified into three different categories. First down situations are divided into first and ten, first and long (more than 10 yards), and first and short (less than 10 yards). Second down situations are broken down into the categories of second and long (more than 6 yards), second and four, five, or six, and second and short (less than 4 yards). Third down situations are third and long (more than 5 yards), third and three, four or five, and third and short (less than 3 yards). Fourth down categories are fourth and long (more than 2 yards), and fourth and one or two yards. (These different categories may be changed as to yardage, according to the desire of the head coach.)

From the play by play, the scout would record each play in its proper category. The running plays would be tabulated according to the hole that was hit. The passes would be shown according to the type of pass, such as roll out pass, drop back pass, play pass, or screen pass.

The "Inside the +10 Yard Line" category would include those plays run from that position on the field. Each line of spaces is to be used for a series of downs within that area. If, for example, a team has first and goal on the +9 yard line, indicate that in the column to the far left. If the first play was run through the 9 hole, you can indicate it with a 1 (first down) in the 9 hole column, together with the play. If the second play is run through

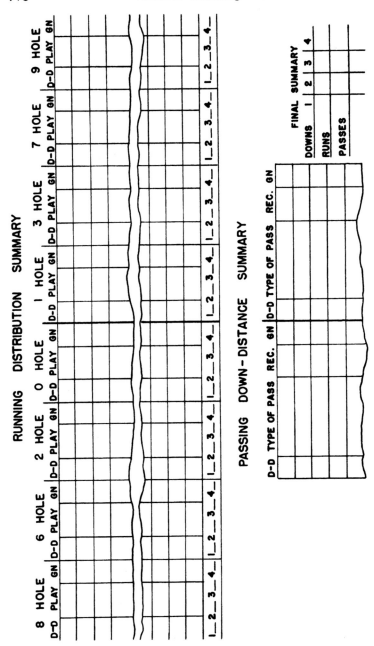

Fig. 9–5. Offensive distribution summary.

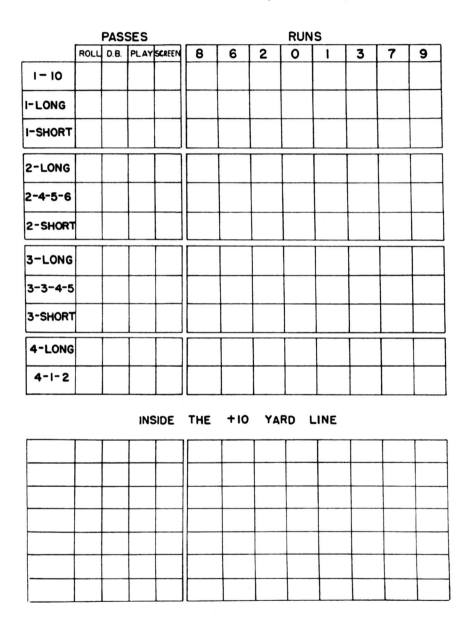

Fig. 9–6. Offensive play distribution and analysis sheet.

the 7 hole, indicate that on the same line with a 2, and the play, in the 7 hole column, etc. If a team has any goal line tendencies, they will readily stand out.

By an analysis such as this, you can get a good idea of what a team might like to do in these situations. This is not to indicate that every team will have strong tendencies in each category, but there are many times when some real tendencies will be uncovered.

There is an analysis of a team's offense that can be made from which, with a quick glance, you can get the hash mark tendencies regardless of formation. It will also show some things not readily apparent in other breakdowns. You can see where on the field a team will begin to throw passes. When a team "limits" its passing zone, knowledge of this fact can affect the defensive quarterback's calls. Some coaches feel that you should not pass until you reach a certain position on the field. (Other coaches, of course, do not agree with this strategy.) You can see where the quarterback likes to throw the ball, and if he has any definite tendencies in regard to throwing screen passes.

The symbols on Fig. 9–7 have the following meanings:

R – Run Right   SR – Screen Right
L – Run Left   SL – Screen Left
PR – Pass Right   K – Kick
PL – Pass Left   QK – Quick Kick
PM – Pass Middle

Some scouts prefer to chart each run with an arrow to show the direction of the run, and indicate the passes with a P and an arrow to show the direction of the pass. Probably a better method would be to show each run with a number correctly identifying the play that was actually run at each particular spot on the field.

A chart similar to the one shown in Fig. 9–7 can be prepared and used to show all plays that were run between the 20 yard line and the goal line at each end of the field. In using the form for this information, the numbers indicating the plays run should be shown on the chart in the approximate area that each play was used. This analysis can show the quarterback's thinking in two critical areas of the playing field.

ANALYSIS OF THE RUNNING PLAYS

After checking the play-by-play worksheets for the play distribution by formations and the various tendencies that may be shown, it is important for you to get on paper the "bread and butter" of the offense. The game material should be closely scrutinized to determine which plays are the basic ones in the team's attack. Determine which plays were used in critical situations, whether successful or not. If the quarterback had faith enough

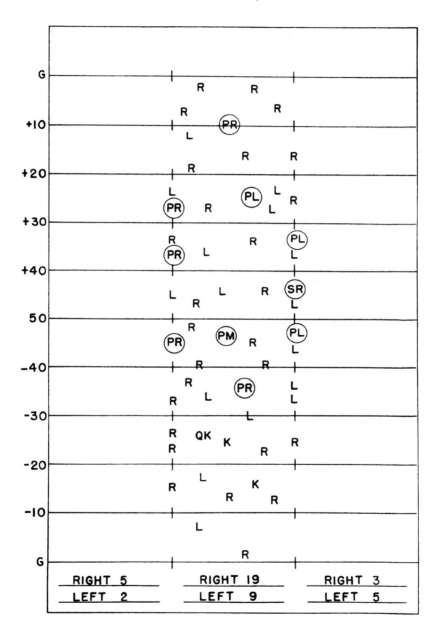

Fig. 9–7. Offensive analysis by field position.

to call them, he must feel that those plays are apt to be the team's best, or that the ball carrier is the strongest and most powerful runner. There might be an indication that several runners are of about equal ability, but that the plays are run through what is probably the strongest part of the offensive line. The running plays that were used most often to hit each hole should be diagramed. If one off-tackle play was run six times and another off-tackle play run only once, it is logical to assume that the quarterback considers the one used the most as a better play. The number of times a play was run and the yardage it gained, or the situation in which it was used, should be the determining factors of the importance that a play has to the offense.

After determining the basic plays of the opponent's attack and drawing each one, the scout should then draw or list the rest of the plays used so that the complete offense can be shown in the scouting report.

Most football teams have favorite formations, and favorite plays from these formations that opponents can, with adequate preparation, remember and adjust to during the ball game. However, there are some teams that have a multitude of formations, and it would be difficult, if not impossible, to teach which plays are the favorites from each formation. There are some teams that have as many, if not more, formations than they have plays. When confronted with this situation, the scout should determine the basic offense of the team by checking the plays run from each formation, and then, after analyzing the offense, condense the formations through the use of some common factors. Such can be done in this manner: Determine what plays have been run to a tight end, regardless of the flanker employed. See what plays were run to the side of a split end (and again, do not consider the flankers). Then each type flanker should be considered to see what plays were run to the tight end and what plays were run to the split end. Often you will find that you will be able to successfully key on the remaining halfback or the fullback.

The defenses employed by your team should adjust easily to all the variations in formations with as few players as possible involved in the adjustments from each defense. The many formations should not be permitted to mask the basic offense. The players should not be concerned with each formation and what plays can be run from each, but rather should know what elements are necessary to employ a phase of the basic offense. For example, an off-tackle play may need the elements of a tight end and the near back in his normal alignment for the key blocks. An end run may have the elements of either a tight or split end and any back flanked to that side. If the key defensive players involved in the play know what elements are necessary for the opponent to employ a "bread and butter" play, they will not be confused by the formations. Many phases of the different formations will be nothing more than "window dressing," and it is important to not be concerned with this camouflage.

ANALYSIS OF THE PASSING PLAYS

By checking your formation distribution charts you can see which are the favorite passing formations, for almost without fail, a team will have a favorite formation for passing. Determine which one has the highest percentage of passes in relation to total plays, and consider that formation the favorite. If a team used a formation thirty-two times and threw ten passes from it, it would not be considered the favorite over a formation used fourteen times, with nine of the plays passes. The formations should be listed in order of passing percentage, and all passes from each formation should be grouped. For example, group all passes from the straight T, those with the right halfback set right, those with the right halfback set left, etc. It is easier to look at the plays in a group by formation and see what passes were thrown, than to list the pass plays in order of preference, regardless of formation.

This grouping also makes it easier for the defensive backs to learn what passes to expect from each formation. If every pass used by the opponent from the straight T formation is run against them in practice, they can get to the point that when the team comes out in that formation, the backs will know what type of pass to expect. The learning procedure is easier when passes are grouped by formation.

Just as there are many ways of charting the running offense, so are there a variety of methods of analyzing the pass offense. One way this may be done is by showing what the down, yardage, hash mark, and position of the field was at each time each particular pass was thrown from a formation. This analysis will often show a definite trend, such as the trends shown in Figs. 9-8 and 9-9.

In Fig. 9-8 you can see that the team threw this pass on a short-yardage situation in its own territory when it had another down to protect its possession of the ball, in case the play was unsuccessful. In Fig. 9-9 you can see that this is a pass thrown as a "possession" type pass. Fairly long yardage was needed to make a first down, and this was the pass selected. The mark through the line showing the pass route of the offensive player indicates to whom the pass was thrown. The receiver is also indicated by the yardage gained figure opposite the point of the arrow, or the "Inc," indicating an incomplete pass.

Another breakdown that some head coaches, and practically all pass defense coaches, want is shown in Fig. 9-10. This shows every pass route taken by each individual receiver from one formation. It not only shows

POSITION	D - D	YD. LINE	GAIN
L	3 – 3	+ 20	INC
L	2 – 2	+ 40	+ 8
M	3 – 1	+ 12	+ 6

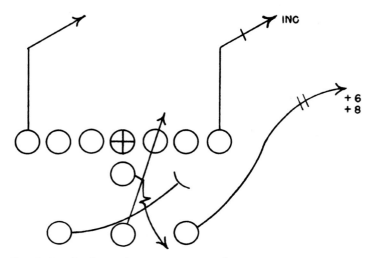

Fig. 9–8. Analysis of a pass pattern—play pass.

all pass routes from one formation, but also to whom the ball was thrown, as well as the yardage gained. In this particular case, the distribution among the two ends and the flanking back is about even. However, in most cases you will find a very uneven distribution, with one particular receiver being on the receiving end of a large percentage of the passes. A favorite receiver undoubtedly would be a factor considered when working on defensive plans, and particularly those of the pass defense.

Some pass defense coaches make up a form similar to the one shown in Fig. 9–10, but showing all pass routes of the receivers, regardless of formation. This type of diagram gives the defenders an opportunity to see the different types of courses that they will confront.

Another form that will show much the same type of information is illustrated in Fig. 9–11. Six squares representing six passing zones are drawn. The vertical lines bisect the center line at the approximate position of the ends in their normal alignment. The horizontal line indicates a depth from the line of scrimmage, in this diagram—10 yards. The area to which each pass was thrown is indicated in its approximate position by denoting the receiver (or intended receiver) with the letters of his position, or if you have a system for numbering the ends and backs, by their respective

POSITION	D – D	YD. LINE	GAIN
M	3 – 8	– 41	+ 9
M	4 – 9	+ 18	INC
L	4 – 10	+ 21	+ 12
L	3 – 9	+ 48	INC

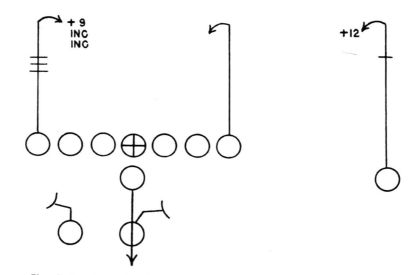

Fig. 9–9. Analysis of a pass pattern—drop back pass.

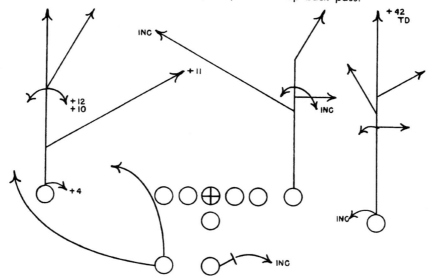

Fig. 9–10. Pass routes of all receivers from one formation.

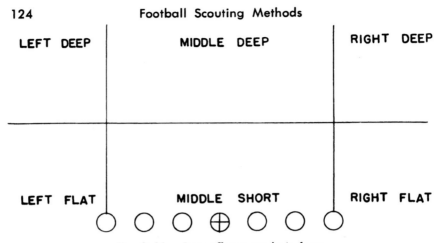

Fig. 9–11.   Pass offense analysis form.

numbers. For example, if the left end is numbered 6 (and the right end 7), you can indicate a pass to him by simply putting his number in the area that the ball was thrown. If the pass was completed, the receiver's number can be circled. It is important that the indication be made in the approximate area of the pass, and not where the receiver was tackled after catching the ball. A separate form can be used for each formation, or one form can be used for all passes. If separate forms are used, the formation can be drawn at the bottom of each page.

The type of analysis shown in Fig. 9–11 could also be used to get hash mark tendencies. The passes thrown, regardless of formation, would be shown on three diagrams representing the three field positions—left hash mark, middle of the field, and right hash mark.

Whichever type of charting is used, you can tell quickly where the team likes to throw the ball, and if there is a favorite receiver, that fact stands out. If such is the case, provisions may be taken to employ a special coverage, or to make an effort to delay him in getting downfield to catch the ball.

In charting the play by play of the game, the scout was instructed to record each substitute entering the game and, if possible, also the player leaving the game. (It is of more importance to note the man entering the game.) One good reason for recording the entrance of the substitute is that there are occasions when a player of some special ability will enter the game for one special play. In looking over your worksheets you will quite often find that the special play is a pass, and if the player has exceptional speed, he may be used to run a deep pattern. This situation may not occur very often during the course of the season, and it may not appear at all, but if a close check is made after every ball game, you may sometimes detect it. Preparation can then be made to be alert for this special weapon, and this preparation could save a touchdown, and possibly a ball game.

Any analysis of a team's pass offense should include an honest appraisal of the passer's ability, as well as the ability of each receiver. By the various analyses made, you can tell if there is a favorite receiver. What are his weapons? Does he rely on speed, maneuverability, size, or desire? It may be possible to double team him in some manner to cut down on his effectiveness. Determine whether the passer can accurately throw the ball long, or if he is strictly a short passer. See how he handled himself when rushed—was he dangerous as a runner, or is there little threat in that respect? What will he do when rushed? How effective is he in finding the receiver who is open?

A beginning scout may question the necessity for so many kinds of analyses and the usefulness of all the information. Perhaps this can best be answered by an example of a real situation in which a tendency was detected—and successfully defensed.

In Terry Brennan's tenure as head coach at Notre Dame, he had a great deal of success with the Split T option play run away from a strong flanker. If Notre Dame was on the right hash mark, it would like to flank the right halfback to the left, or the wide side of the field, in hopes that the defense would rotate its backs to this flanker. Since most teams were employing a two-deep defense, that was a customary adjustment to this type of flanker. If the defense did rotate to the flanker, Notre Dame would run the quarterback option into the sideline with a great deal of success. This put a heavy burden on the defensive end, since he did not have a corner back to help him. If, however, the defense did not rotate, the quarterback would check off to a fullback sweep to the left, or wide side of the field.

By looking at a formation and play distribution analysis such as shown in Figs. 9–1 or 9–2, it was not apparent that most of Notre Dame's long gains from these two plays came from the above situation (or the reverse of it when Notre Dame was on the left hash mark). By utilizing the method of analysis shown in Fig. 9–3, however, the reason for success became apparent. These same plays were run from the middle of the field, but in many instances to less advantage than when run from the hash marks.

Navy spent considerable time working against hash mark tendencies, and usually this proved very beneficial. One of Eddie Erdelatz' (and Dick Duden's) theories of defense was to present a defensive alignment that made it uninviting for the opponent to run the plays with which it had previously had great success. If, for instance, a team was successful with a play such as a sweep to the right with the right halfback set right, and the team showed little or nothing back to the left, either running or passing, from that formation, Navy would not hesitate to rotate the backfield to the flanker when confronted with that formation. This would present the quarterback, as well as the coach, of that team with the picture of running against a stacked defense. There would be two alternatives: (1) continue to run a play which worked well in the past, or (2) have the quarterback check off at the line of scrimmage. In either of these situations, the opponent was at a disadvantage. In the first case, the team would be running against a defense that was adjusted to be strong against that play. In the second case, it would be required to do something that college teams seldom do well, and that is automatic or check off to new plays at the line of scrimmage. Eleven football players are involved in this change, and the chance for error is definitely present.

However, the Notre Dame sequence presented a different kind of problem for Navy in that Notre Dame had good plays to both directions. If you rotated or stacked your defense to the flanker, the play could go the other direction with something proven successful, the quarterback option play. If you did not rotate your defense, the quarterback could pitch the ball to the fullback, who would run a sweep toward the flanker, with probable gain. When faced with this situation, a new kind of solution was required. Eddie Erdelatz was, while coaching college football, the leading exponent of slanting, looping, and stunting defenses. By virtue of the type of defense that he coached, he was able to devise one that was effective against Notre Dame.

If Notre Dame came out of the huddle with the right halfback flanked left, and Navy had a slant to Notre Dame's right called, the backfield would rotate to the flanker. This would give the appearance of making the quarterback option play inviting. On the snap of the ball, the line would slant away from the flanker, toward the direction of the play. The linebackers were assigned to go with the quarterback, and thus there was help for the defensive end. The linebacker was assigned to take the quarterback, with help from the tackle and middle guard, if possible. The defensive end would then have the responsibility to take the left halfback, if the ball was pitched out by the quarterback.

If, in the same alignment, there was a slant left called, the backfield would not rotate to the flanker. This would appear to make the fullback sweep the best play to run. Again, on the snap of the ball, the Navy line would be slanting in the direction of the play and would be in an excellent position to defend against the sweep. In one defense the line would slant toward the flanker, and in the other, the line would slant away from the flanker. In both situations, the defenses were sound and effective.

This is an example of one way to combat a tendency that has been successful for a team, once that tendency has been established. The tendency may not even be apparent in one kind of analysis, but it may show up if a different approach is used. If a scout continues to use different methods and approaches, and does some experimenting, he will eventually be rewarded by the detection of something of importance.

The information condensed into the offensive part of the scouting report should show in complete form what the opposing team has done, both running and passing, from each formation. Therefore, it is this information which should determine what defensive adjustments should be made, or whether new defenses are needed to combat the strength of the opponent. Such concrete knowledge of an opponent's previous offense should be the basis of defensive game planning—not what a team *might* do, or what it *should have* done or *could have* done in past games. Of equal, if not more, importance is the fact that this knowledge should be passed on to your players in such a manner that they thoroughly understand it, can absorb it, and use it to advantage.

The defensive signal callers should be made aware of the tendencies of the opposing team by chalk talks or meetings with members of the coaching staff. The knowledge obtained in these meetings should be the basis for calling defenses during the game. To enhance the learning process, charts can be prepared to be put in the dressing room to be studied by the players. The important factor here is that each player should try to learn only those tendencies that affect his particular position, and not get confused by attempting to absorb all of the opponent's tendencies from all formations. If an opposing team likes to run off tackle from a certain formation, your ends, tackles and linebacker on that side should be cognizant of this. The pass defenders should know from what formations the opponent prefers to pass. If there is any tip-off as to where a play may be going, the players directly concerned should be alert for it. Other players should be aware of any specific conditions affecting their individual positions.

On the field, the team should work against the strong plays from each formation the opponent used. Everything done in this respect should resemble as closely as possible the way the opponents do it. The opponent's plays should be drawn on cards so that a freshman, Junior Varsity, or "B" team can run them in the correct manner. Some coaches put the corresponding numbers of the opponents on the key players of these "scout" teams so that the varsity can become familiar with them, and can more quickly recognize the various formations.

When sufficient players are available, sometimes two distinct teams will be used to work against the varsity. One team will specialize in the opponent's running offense, while the other will work on the passing game. By having two teams, each can become more proficient and consequently can present a better picture of the opponents. When this is possible, it becomes much easier and quicker to teach the various defensive adjustments to combat the strengths of the opponent. The line can then work as a unit against one team, and the backs can work against the other. The line should have the opportunity to work alone against the running game in order to get as familiar as possible with the opposition's attack. The defensive backs can work against the pass patterns of the opponent. In order to better teach the backs what to expect, all the passes should be run from one formation before going on to another. When they have seen what to expect from the various formations, the remaining practices on pass defense during the week should be concerned with the favorite and most dangerous passes. The ball should be worked from hash mark to hash mark. Sometime during the week, they should also work against passes near the goal line.

After all the defensive alignments are learned, your line and backs should work together as a team. During the latter part of the week some time should be devoted to "situations," with the "scout" team representing the opponent's offense. This offensive team can start close to the goal line and work from the formations and running plays used by the opponent in prior games, as reported in the scouting report. A coach can call the "situations" as the team moves down the field, working from hash mark to hash mark. "Situations" called should include all that can reasonably be expected during a game. The "scout" team should run the plays that the opponent has favored in those situations and the defensive signal caller should try to make the best defensive call to combat the strength of each particular play. The offensive team can be called upon to punt so that punt rushes or returns can also be practiced. Goal line plays can be emphasized for a period to adequately cover them. Some time should also be spent working against the Point After Touchdown or the two-point plays.

Additional "situations" of score and time can be added to teach your team to quickly make the proper defensive calls. If the offensive team is "losing," and it is late in the game, then a Prevent or victory defense will undoubtedly be used to prevent the long pass completion.

Late in the week, possibly Thursday after practice, or Friday, a written test can be given to the players. This test should be short, and the questions asked should be those that the coach of each particular phase of the game feels the individual players should know. Formations can be drawn and the players asked to list the favorite and dangerous plays from them. Defensive backs can be asked which players other than the quarterback have thrown passes. Or, when the quarterback has used play action passes, and from what type of faking, and so on. The questions should be relatively simple, but yet cover the important phases of the opponent's offense. The test should cover such basic material that all of the players will get a perfect score. If, however, some questions are missed, the coach should go over them with the players involved.

It is important that the players know as much about the opponent as possible. It is better, however, to give them the important information and have them learn it thoroughly, rather than give them a great deal, all of which they cannot absorb. A coach's ability is not judged on what *his* knowledge of the game is, but rather on what he can impart to his players. Knowledge learned on the field appears to be more meaningful than that obtained in chalk talks or lectures. The two methods may, however, be combined with success, but provisions should be made to devote some of the practice sessions to some form of simulated game conditions as anticipated from the opponent as a result of scouting reports.

10

The Final Report

The information obtained in scouting the opponent should be condensed into a final report. The final report form shown in the Appendix can be used to report a single game and can also be used for the composite report of all the games scouted. Of course, more information will be shown in a composite report than in the report of a single game. The form and content of a final report can vary a great deal, depending on the desires of the head coach. The report form shown here is designed to fulfill the requirements of a particular coach, but in general it covers all of the main phases of any final report. Regardless of the form you choose, the objective of your final scouting report should be the organization of your material in such a way that you can easily present the pertinent information to your coaching staff and players. This presentation of information can be accomplished by submitting both a written and an oral report to the coaches and players. The same type of report can be given to each group, but the degree of detail will vary. In both instances, the scout can be subjected to questions in order to clarify or detail any phase of his report.

Most of the charts in this particular final report form have been explained and commented on in the previous chapters dealing with the analysis of the defense and the analysis of the offense. The other pages in the report are self-explanatory. This report is to be completed after each game scouted; the same report form is used for compiling a composite of several games, with additional forms also utilized to show the various tendencies. These additional forms are prepared on large, white, 11 × 14-inch cards. The use of cards is recommended so that these forms may be used independently of the report by either coaches or players, and should be of such a size that the diagrams and figures can be easily interpreted in group viewing. (Such cards can also be posted in the locker room to be studied by the players.)

With the specialization in football coaching at the present time, it seems advisable to have the final report prepared in two separate parts, with one part devoted entirely to the offensive phases of the game and the other part covering the defensive phases. When two scouts are used in scouting a team, it would be simple to divide the responsibility and have one coach prepare the phase of the report dealing with the offense and the other coach prepare the defensive phase of the report. Then, in studying the final report, the offensive and defensive coaches could simultaneously concern themselves with their respective responsibilities.

The information contained in any report must meet the test of being of value in formulating game plans, or in better preparing an individual or the team to compete against another player or team. Many head coaches, for example, will ask to have each player listed by name, number, height, weight, class, and position. Some of this information is of value, but much of it is not. The names and numbers of the good and poor football players certainly should be noted. The numbers of the remaining players might also be designated by position. The height, weight, and class do not, in themselves, tell one thing about a player's athletic ability. There are good small football players and poor big football players. Personally, it is felt that information of this type might sometimes be beneficial only as a psychological weapon. In checking with the players on this, it was found to be practically unanimous that they considered height, weight, and class of little interest and of no value to them. As one head coach so aptly put it, "If we can't do anything about it, don't bother me with needless statistics or comments on it." This might well be the basis for your selection of any information to be submitted in a scouting report.

There are several methods that can be used to present the scouting report to the members of the coaching staff. Often the make-up of the staff, their experience in coaching, and the division of responsibility among the coaches will be determining factors. One method that has a great deal of merit is to have the scout present the report orally, much like a professor or teacher giving a class lecture. The composite of all information obtained (both from scouting and the study of movies) is the source for the information presented. As the various phases of the game are covered, each coach takes notes on the information given which affects his coaching responsibility. (Those coaches who have the press box and bench duties on the day of the game will want to be familiar with all that the opponent does.) The defensive coaches would, of course, be primarily concerned with the offensive formations and distribution, tendencies, tip-offs, offensive personnel, and the phases of the kicking game that affect the defense. The offensive coaches would take note of the defenses anticipated, the adjustments of those defenses, defensive tendencies, and the phases of the kicking game affecting the offense.

As the scouting report is presented, the coaches can ask questions of the scout to further detail or clarify any part of the report. Each coach is responsible for obtaining the answers to questions that will directly concern him, and he is held accountable for knowing that part of the report. It has been found more meaningful for a coach to write down those phases of the report that concern him. This is not to infer that each coach is going to take verbatim notes on what the scout presents, but rather that the coach will record and know the parts of the report important to him. Each defensive coach, for example, should record each formation and the plays that are run from each. The defensive coaches should also take note of the important tendencies, the strong and weak personnel, etc. Any information necessary to formulating game plans should be available to each coach, as this eliminates constantly referring to the scouting report in order to settle a point of discussion.

This system can be altered slightly. It may be advantageous to have some sheets of the report mimeographed and in the hands of each coach as the oral report is given. The coaches can then see the distribution by formation, for example, as it is being discussed. Other sheets might show the tendencies offensively, or the run-down on the personnel. Since the coaches will already have the information in hand as it is being discussed, they will need to only make notes and comments on each phase as the scout reports it.

It is also possible to prepare a report outlining the important information, and give a copy to each coach to follow as the complete report is given orally. When such a written report is used, it will be very much like the one given to the players, but will include greater detail. Regardless of what method is used in presenting the final report, the scout should be available to answer questions, and his final composite report should be available for the coaches to study and refer to.

If a written report is to be made up for the players, it should be brief and concise, but yet contain important and useful information. This report should not be loaded with a lot of details that will only tend to confuse the players and make the report uninteresting for them to read, and difficult to remember and absorb. Most reports start out with a statement about the opponent telling of the team's record and accomplishments, outstanding players, and some statement calculated to "fire up" the players reading it. If the opponent is strong, the statement tends to play down the record. If the record is poor, the scout mentions all the tough breaks the opponent has had that can account for the poor record.

The opening statement is usually followed by a run-down on the personnel, with emphasis on the strong and weak players.

The favorite running plays are then diagramed, and proper comments are made about them—such as, "these are preferred on short yardage," or, "these are favorite goal-line plays," etc. Similar information is given about the pass plays, together with comments.

The offensive information is generally followed by a page or so devoted to the defenses the opponent has used, and the adjustments made—with a special notation on short-yardage and goal-line defenses.

The report is then concluded with remarks about the kicking game and a final statement about the team.

The oral report to the players should follow the same outline as the written report, in regard to the opponent. If the opponent is tough and has a good record, the scout should make an effort to play down the record, but he must make sure not to do it to the point of being ridiculous. You can attribute some of the success to luck, some to breaks, and, of course, most to the fact that it is a good football team, but one that can be beaten with maximum effort. You must be honest in your appraisal, but don't make the opponent sound invincible.

On the other hand, if the opposition's record is not too good, you will want to caution your players against being upset by taking that opponent too lightly. If at all possible, bring out some extenuating circumstances to which you may attribute the poor record. Such circumstances could have been key injuries, unfortunate breaks going against the team, or a really tough schedule.

In going over what the other team does, the emphasis should be not so much on *what* it does, but rather the team's method of doing it. Go over the team's favorite plays and show how the players block them, and how they try to handle the defensive men at the point of attack. If the team has an end run that has been successful, and the blocking is hooking the defensive end with the offensive end, emphasize such to your ends. If the halfback is to block the end, and the halfback "cheats" in lining up so he can get to the end quicker, caution your ends to look for that, and to be alert for it. Go over all the opponent's key plays and alert the defensive men involved.

When discussing the pass offense, go into detail on the favorite passes, and mention when the team likes to throw them, who the favorite receivers are, etc. Make it a personal message from you to the player or players involved. It is good to call some of the players by name, and put certain things to them as a challenge between those players and the opposing men. Make every effort to get your team alert to the things that the opponent does well. To me, this is one great advantage that an oral report has over a written report—you can get the personal touch in it, as well as the challenge. Also, if you diagram various things the opponent does, and discuss them as you diagram them, they tend to become more meaningful to the players, and consequently are better remembered.

When movies of a previous game of the opponent are available, these can be shown after the scout's oral report to the players. The scout points out examples of the plays, blocking, etc. that were covered in his report, and this serves to emphasize their importance, and makes it easier for the players to remember the information in the report. Whatever presentation of his material a scout prefers, he must make sure that it is comprehensible to the players.

11

Self-scouting
and Postgame Analysis

The self-scouting of a football team should start when the team is organized. All football teams do some self-scouting, although they may not think of it in those terms. When the players are appraised, compared, graded, and coached, a certain degree of self-scouting is taking place. However, real scouting should begin as soon as a team begins to put in the offense and defense.

As the plays are put into the offense, the actions of the backs should be charted to make sure that one back will not lead the defense to the direction of the play or the point of attack. This step is taken to insure that the offense is such that there are no definite tip-offs by the restricted actions of some of the players, notably the backs. It might be well to analyze your offense from the action of the various backs. It is not unusual, in many instances, to find that the direction of the play can be determined by the first step of one of the halfbacks or the fullback. For example, on some teams any time the fullback goes up the middle, the ball is given to him; there is never a fake to him, with a hand-off to another back hitting a different hole. From an offensive alignment of the normal T formation, the offense of many teams is such that the action of the fullback will key the direction of the play. Other teams will give a definite key by the action of one of the halfbacks. When either of these situations occurs and is detected, the linebackers can key on the backs, and can move much more quickly in the direction of the play than they could if there were no tip-off.

In an offense where one back is flanked, it is not unusual to find the remaining halfback a good key in determining very quickly the direction of the flow. If the halfback goes right, the play goes anywhere to the right of center, depending on the action of the fullback. As this is often the case, the linebackers can move quickly and can cover holes that they might not ordinarily be able to cover. An example of this is shown in Fig. 11–1,

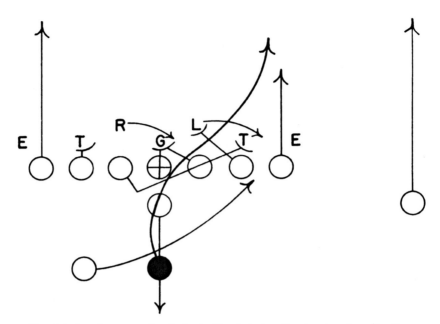

Fig. 11-1. An example of the halfback being the key to play direction.

in which the left halfback was a perfect key to the direction of the play. The linebackers played it as shown.

On several occasions at Navy in the past four years, Navy's linebackers keyed on the left halfback in similar situations. If, on another play, the fullback did not come up the middle, the left linebacker would be able to react to the outside faster, as would the right linebacker.

It would have been a simple matter for the offense to run the same play and swing the left halfback left, and thus destroy that key, or the left halfback could set up as he would on pass protection. If the same play would be run to the other side of the line, trapping the defensive right tackle, then it might be well to run it as shown in Fig. 11-2. This would also break the key.

At the Naval Academy during the last six years, the linebackers have had as their keys, on different occasions, the left halfback, the fullback, the remaining halfback when one was flanked, the spin of the quarterback, and the guards. The offensive plays of the opponent were diagramed, and each back was checked to see if he would lead the linebackers in the direction of the play by the direction of his initial move. If there was one play where the key was not true, such a key was not used. It is possible that in a normal T formation one back, such as the fullback, would be the key, and on an-

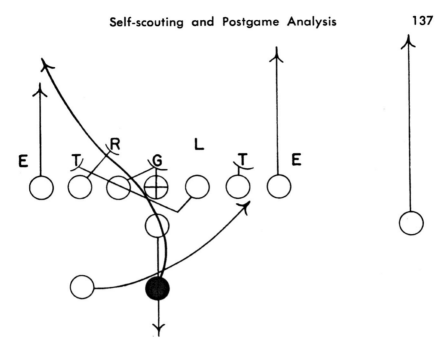

Fig. 11—2. An example of the halfback destroying the key to play direction.

other formation, such as one in which a back was flanked, the remaining halfback would be the key. If counter plays are not a main part of a team's attack, the scout should investigate the actions of the backs to see if one of them will lead to the direction of the play.

Most coaches will have a thorough study of their films made by the assistants as soon after a game as is possible. However, in most cases the study is only a form of grading individual players to determine their knowledge of assignments and efficiency in carrying them out. Unquestionably, this is a valuable coaching aid and is important in the selection of team members. But there is a great deal more useful information that can be obtained with relatively few work hours added to those already put in by the coaches involved.

This additional study and analysis can be an effective way of determining the efficiency of your own scouting, as well as a way of getting additional information on your opponent that can be used for future reference. You can also get an idea of how well your opponents scouted you, and their resourcefulness in game planning. In order to be of value, a study such as this should be made as soon after the game as possible so that the results can be interpreted, and measures taken to utilize the information obtained. How detailed the work will be will depend upon the wishes of the head coach, the amount of time and coaches available to do the work, as well as the equipment needed. If the study is to be tied in with the grading of player personnel, much of the information necessary to make an effective analysis of your team as well as that of the opponent would be available from this grading. The forms used in this study should show the formation, play, defense used, and the gain. A form similar to the one shown in Fig. 4–4 can be used.

If grading the players is not part of the coaching practice used at your particular school, the same forms can be used, one for each team, and a complete breakdown of a game can be obtained in much less time than many coaches realize. Two coaches can be assigned to chart the play by play, one coach for each team, to get the information desired. It is preferable to have the coach who scouted the opponent chart the team that he scouted, while another member of the staff charts your own team. The coach that is charting the opponent will need a pad or tablet to diagram plays and defenses, and to record any other pertinent information that cannot be shown on the worksheet.

By making a self-analysis of your team, you can often get considerable knowledge that could be beneficial, and possibly something vital enough to be the difference between winning and losing some games. It is common knowledge that opponents are scouting your team to get information and to establish the various tendencies that may appear. Unless you put what your team is doing into some graphic form, it is not always possible to realize exactly what habits your team may be getting into. Undoubtedly, the grading of the playing personnel has a great deal of merit, but too often such grading is not carried out to the point where it shows the different things about your team that your opponents know, or should know. You can, in reality, make out a scouting report on your own team which will show what your players do, and when they do it. One of the first things a coach can do is to make a formation distribution chart. This would show the plays that were run from each formation and the success of each play. Generally, all the formations used in one game can be put on a single 8 × 11-inch white card, together with the play distribution from each formation. Either of the forms shown in Figs. 9–1 and 9–2 to chart formation and play distribution can be used. In order to show a more graphic picture that can be interpreted at a glance, it is recommended that different colors be used to show each different back carrying the ball.

As the season progresses, this procedure can be carried further, and a week-by-week composite of all formations and the distribution from each of them can be made. Such a composite can be put on a 24 × 36-inch card, or separate 8 × 11-inch cards can be used for each formation. If a 24 × 36-inch card is used, it can be put on the wall, and at a glance the coaches can get a complete picture of your offense as it has been run to date. The same procedure is used in making this composite as is used in preparing the individual game card. Underneath each formation, each type of pass used can be listed under the various types of pass protection used, together with the success of each play. By the use of abbreviations or some code, you can show the completions with a figure indicating the gain, the (—) symbol can show the incomplete passes, and the letter I can indicate interceptions. This part of the chart is shown in Fig. 11–3.

50 Passes	60 Passes	70 Passes	Play Passes
Hook (—) 9,8,11	X 14, 12, 18	Swing Y 16	27 X (—)
I, 10	Ban Y I, 14	Stop I	29 P 36

Fig. 11–3. A composite showing the passes from a formation.

It takes much less space to show the passes if abbreviations are used. Care should be taken to allow ample room to show all the passes that might be thrown throughout the course of the season. All the information, both running and passing, about a formation, as used to date, is shown. Then if you see any strong tendencies developing, it is possible to make some adjustments in your offense. Naturally, you will want to continue to run successful plays, but it is possible that such could be run from various formations, and thus any key would be destroyed. The gain of any play that scored a touchdown can be circled. And, if so desired, a complete efficiency rating on each play used can be kept.

Any analysis that is made of an opponent as part of the scouting report can be made of your own team with a minimum of additional work. Down and distance summaries can be made to see what, if any, tendencies you have in that area. The form shown in Fig. 9–4 can be used for this purpose. This can be a valuable aid in quarterback instruction meetings, and can be used as a check to see how well the quarterbacks carried out the games plans as prescribed to them. It is possible to tell whether successful plays were called as often as they should have been, or if short gainers were called too frequently. Such a down and distance summary can also be used as a valuable check on the quarterbacks' habits. They often get into a set pattern of calling certain plays in certain situations, and this should be altered so that the opponent will not know what to expect. An analysis of your team's offensive play distribution, as shown in the form in Fig. 9–6, could also be helpful in this area, as well as some study on hash mark tendencies.

Whenever possible, a composite of all games to date should be made after each contest has been analyzed. The cards and forms to be used can be prepared prior to the season, and since most coaches have some type of breakdown made of each game—used either to grade the players or to evaluate the plays—this information can be transposed to the proper chart with a minimum of time and effort. It does not require a mound of papers and hours of sorting, but rather a matter of a short time to record each play and gain on the proper chart.

The same type studies that are made of the team offensively can be made of the team's defense. By going through the movies and getting the down and distance, the defense, the play, and its success, some excellent studies can be made of your defense. You can tell where each defense was attacked, and the strength and weakness of each. It may become apparent that a great deal of yardage is being gained at a certain spot, a fact which could lead to additional instruction and practice for the players involved.

The same approach can be used in determining in what areas the opponents have thrown and completed each pass. A form such as shown in Fig. 9–11 is used. Each pass is indicated as complete, incomplete, or intercepted, and, if possible, the responsibility is charged to a player or players on all completions. This has been a basis for part of the teaching procedure of Rick Forzano, the pass defense coach at the Naval Academy. If one player is found to be charged with a number of completions out of line with those of the other defenders, that player will undoubtedly be the recipient of additional coaching. The number of completions charged against each defensive player, as well as the number of interceptions, is posted in the locker room. If two players are equally responsible, then each is charged with a one-half completion. This type of study is not always possible if adequate movies are not available. It is almost essential that wide-angle movies be used for the coach to be able to determine the pass completion responsibility, but wide-angle movies are not necessary to know the approximate area of completion.

Any and all notes, diagrams, defenses, and ready lists used for a particular game should be kept for future reference. If the opponent is to be met the following year, regardless of what success you had against that team, make a note of the postgame thoughts that the coaches express. Almost without fail, a coach will say, "If we were playing that team again next Saturday, there are a few things that I would do differently." Make some notes on postgame thoughts, as those same ideas could be of value the following year. Quite often too many details and thoughts are left to memory, and after a period of time, it is not unusual to find that our memory is not as retentive as we would like it to be. Even though the same opponent may not be on the schedule for the following year, all material on the opponent should be kept because the same defensive thinking may be of value against some other opponent which employs a similar offense.

THE POSTGAME ANALYSIS OF THE OPPONENT

If time is not the determining factor, a scouting report should be made out on the opponent the week after a game is played. It is more advantageous to do it at this time, rather than at the end of the season, since everything about the game is still fresh in the scout's mind. It will give the scout an opportunity to appraise his own work, and will also give him a better idea of the thinking and capabilities of the other team and the coaches. This is actually the first time that you can properly evaluate the opponent with something you know a great deal about—your own team. The other teams that played your opponent were, for the most part, complete strangers to the scout.

One of the easiest and best ways to appraise the game plans of an opponent is to compare them with your ideas of how you would plan to play against your own team, on the basis of the knowledge that you had of your own players and their offensive and defensive capabilities. Unquestionably, you should know more about your own team than any opponent should know, but how the opposing coaches planned the game should give you an idea of whether they were on the right track or not. Did they concentrate their passing attack on your weakest defender, or did they throw passes just because the situation called for a long-yardage gainer? Did they try to trap your most trapable linemen, or did they try to trap everybody on the line, running trap plays indiscriminately? Did they concentrate their running game at the weakest linemen? If they kept hitting you where you were the weakest, you must give them credit for excellent preparation and must respect them for it in the future.

By using the same standards for scouting the opponent in your game as were used in the games that were scouted prior to your game, you can get a very good idea of the amount of special preparation that was made for your game. This kind of knowledge is invaluable to you in the future, as it can help you to anticipate what may be expected of that team. Any study or analysis of a game played should include a great many notes, since this material will be used for reference in the future, and nothing should be left to memory. It should be remembered that what is common knowledge about a team shortly after you play against it will very often need the assistance of notes and diagrams to be correctly recalled in the future. It is also especially important to make a close study of each defense and the adjustments from the defenses to the various flankers. All of this information should be kept on file for future reference.

If time is a great factor and a postgame analysis of the opponent cannot be made the week after the game, it certainly must be done at the end of the season.

SELF-ANALYSIS OF HIGH SCHOOL TEAMS

Quite often high school coaches do not have the finances available to take movies of games that can be studied in the detail desired. Much of the information discussed, therefore, is not available to some high school coaches. Another factor that must be considered is that often they do not get their movies from the processor as soon as they would like, and as a result, they do not have the opportunity (before the next game) to incorporate their findings, to correct their mistakes, or to take advantage of information obtained, even if the movies are adequate. If this is the situation, then other measures can and should be taken, although none of them will even remotely approach the results that can be obtained from studying good movies. However, it is possible to get important information that will give you a fairly accurate picture of your offense and will be helpful in future planning.

One method is to have a former player, or an injured player, keep a running account of the game, using a form that would have space to record the formation, play, and the gain. Such information can be used by the head coach as a possible basis for second-half offensive plans. At the conclusion of the game, a tabulation can be made to give a statistical value to each play. Information of this kind could also be used as a basis for instructions to the quarterback, and for the coach to appraise his offense.

Another method of obtaining some of the same information, as well as additional knowledge about your team, is to have some individual who has an interest and knowledge of the game scout your team. In many localities there are high schools that play their games on different days and do not play each other. A mutual arrangement between coaches can be made wherein a coach can scout another coach's team and the second coach can reciprocate. An arrangement of this type can be mutually helpful and beneficial. It is good to know what other coaches see in your team; very often they can see things that you are not aware of. There are many college coaches in the country who have their own team scouted by a professional scout in order to get an impartial report, because very often a coach will have a slanted impression of his own team. This same practice can be followed in high schools. A scouting report on a coach's own team could possibly bring out impressions on some phases of the game that have unintentionally been neglected. It can be helpful to know what other coaches notice, since it is practically impossible to look at your own team objectively.

A variation of this procedure comes to mind—one that in this case proved very helpful to a college. As part of the curriculum in Physical Education, a course in football was offered in which the various phases of the game were taught by members of the varsity coaching staff. A part of this course was devoted to scouting, and in order to give the pupils some practical experience, they were assigned to scout the varsity home games. At the conclusion of a game, each student compiled his report, and the following week the reports were discussed in class. Through these reports the head coach was amazed to learn of the number of definite offensive patterns that his team had developed, which, if not altered somewhat, could have been utilized to great advantage by future opponents. This scouting report by inexperienced student scouts showed some things so conclusively that it led to the alteration of one pattern of play. A particular running play was used often in a short-yardage situation. A pass play incorporating the fake of the running play was added to the offense. In the next game this pass play was used in a short-yardage situation and scored a touchdown. The outcome of the game was decided by one touchdown, so the importance of this change in pattern by the addition of a play is obvious.

Often simple alterations can be made in offensive plans to destroy some of the patterns that have been established. This was brought home forcefully during the 1960 season at the Naval Academy. In checking over the play distribution from the various formations prior to the game with Southern Methodist University, it was found that we were developing some strong play tendencies from several formations. The plays could have been run from other formations but they had not been, simply because the quarterbacks got into a set pattern. This was pointed out to the quarterbacks and the ready lists (plays to be run from each formation) were changed to alter the pattern. The results showed that our most successful plays in that game were the ones run from formations from which they had never been run in prior games.

At times it is amazing to see the extremes to which coaches will go to get information on an opponent through scouting and the study of movies. This same effort is often carried on to the study of individual players on the team and their grading by the use of a complicated system. But yet little or no effort is expended in getting impressions of their own team, either other people's or even their own, through some method of self-scouting. All coaches are aware of the fact that their opponents are scouting them, and it seems logical to assume that the opponents are getting information and impressions. This information is available and can easily be gotten on one's own team, and if it is obtained it can be used to advantage.

12

Tip-offs

Most of a scout's efforts and observations should be centered on getting the specific information desired by the head coach, as detailed in the final report. However, as the scout gains in experience and proficiency, and particularly when he has the opportunity to observe the same team more than once, he may begin to look for some less obvious things. Before a play starts, a scout can watch the players closely to see if he might detect some tip-off that may be of value, either in game planning or in helping an individual or individuals in their play against that opponent. It is not unusual to detect something that a player does which will foretell his actions during the play. This, of course, can be of some value. It is most unusual to find a key individual who will foretell what the team will do (by tipping-off the whole play) before the actual play starts. This type of knowledge would be of great value. Although it is generally difficult for the scout to detect tip-offs because he is concentrating on other phases of the game, there are areas to which the proficient scout may look to uncover opponent's idiosyncrasies, ones which will predict the forthcoming action. Some actual tip-offs will be discussed in this chapter to illustrate what a scout might look for (and also to show that some of the better football teams and players can and do, inadvertently, become the victims of habit).

The positioning of a football player's feet has led to some interesting tip-offs. Knowledge of a certain player's changing the position of his feet to better carry out his assignment has been used to definite advantage by several teams, since it was a foolproof tip-off as to the action forthcoming not only from that player, but from the team as well. This is one area in which close observation of a player's habits could pay excellent dividends.

This was first brought to the author's attention while coaching at Vanderbilt University. At that time the scouting assignments were set up so that a coach would have the same team to scout every year. It was each coach's responsibility to scout "his" team at least three times, if the schedule permitted it, and to make a thorough study of that team in the off-season. John Clark, one of the assistant coaches and a former captain at Vanderbilt, was assigned to scout the University of Mississippi and got to know "Ole Miss" quite well as a team. He was familiar with that team's kind of football and tendencies, and was proficient as well, so he was able to look for some of the little things that might be tip-offs and could be used to advantage. By concentrating on the foot alignment of different players prior to the start of each play, he was able to detect that the quarterback would line up with his feet parallel on some occasions, while on others his feet would be staggered. After closer scrutiny, he found that when the quarterback lined up to take the ball from center and his feet were staggered, the play was a drop-back pass every time. Evidently, the quarterback felt that he could drop back faster with his feet in this position. When the quarterback took his position to receive the snap and had his feet parallel, it was a running play every time. The scout continued to observe the quarterback prior to every play, and found the tip-off to be foolproof every time.

"Ole Miss" was to play Kentucky the week prior to meeting Vanderbilt. It happened that Kentucky had obtained the same knowledge about the idiosyncrasies of the "Ole Miss" quarterback. The Kentucky coaches studied movies of games prior to the one in which the tip-off was first noted, and found it to be a true one every time. Kentucky was hoping that this would not be detected by the "Ole Miss" coaches before the game with Kentucky, and of course Vanderbilt coaches were wishing that the tip-off would stand up for two weeks. As it turned out, the tip-off did hold true for Kentucky, and the Kentucky team was able to intercept six passes and run them back for a total yardage that is still the NCAA record.

Kentucky found that the stagger of the quarterback's feet was so noticeable that it was easily detected by the linemen. The linemen, in turn, then gave a verbal signal that alerted the whole team to a pass. The Kentucky team could then be ready for the pass, which is exactly what the "Ole Miss" quarterback called. This tip-off was a contributing factor in Kentucky's beating "Ole Miss."

After the game, Coach Clark talked with the Kentucky coaches, who were convinced that "Ole Miss" was not aware of the tip-off. They felt that Vanderbilt would also be able to capitalize on that same tip-off. The Vanderbilt coaches and players went into their game, hoping that the tip-off would still hold true, but realizing it was possible "Ole Miss" had become aware of the quarterback's habit and had corrected it, or that some Kentucky players might have mentioned it after the game to some players from Mississippi. Very early in Vanderbilt's game, it became obvious that the quarterback lined up the same way on every play, and the valuable tip-off was now useless. Fortunately, Vanderbilt was able to beat "Ole Miss," but it would have been much easier if Vanderbilt had always known when to expect a pass. Kentucky's being able to capitalize on the tip-off was a forceful lesson in the importance of a scout's checking the positioning of the feet of football players. But Vanderbilt's game was also a valuable lesson—in teaching that you cannot base your entire game plans on a tip-off of this nature, but must have alternative plans to use in the event the tip-off does not hold up for your game.

Many football teams will have some player on the team who will alter his stance slightly to get into a more comfortable or advantageous position to carry out an assignment. There have been many instances in which it has been noticed that an individual has changed his stance, but since the player involved was not a key individual, such knowledge benefited only the player who lined up opposite him. It has not been a common occurrence to find a key player (such as a quarterback) who would tip-off the team's next play.

The 1958 Army football team was certainly one of the country's finest, and must be considered as well a coached and drilled football team as the author has ever scouted. Army had an excellent offense that was new to college football in the way that it was executed. The "Lonely End" offense created some diversionary thought among football coaches, but it was no mere psychological "gimmick"—the offense in itself had that wonderful balance between running and passing that makes defensing it extremely difficult. Army's defense was also effective. The team's defensive line play was quick, agile, and basically predicated on slanting, some looping, deals and stunts between linemen and linebackers, or between various linemen. But as well drilled as the players were, they gave a tip-off as to what they were going to do basically on defense. Every time they got into a defensive alignment, it was possible to determine which way some of the players were going to slant, therefore you could tell which holes the linebackers were responsible to cover. Regardless of who was playing in the line, there was a tip-off in every instance. This whole pattern became evident simply through checking one man on defense. This led to further checks on other defensive men. When the fullback was up on the line of scrimmage, it was possible to know the defensive moves of four of the six defensive linemen, and from this you could have excellent knowledge of what responsibilities the linebackers had. When Army was in its Oklahoma 5–4 alignment, one player telegraphed the movements of the middle guard and one tackle.

One of Army's basic defenses employed bringing the fullback up on the line of scrimmage as the defensive end. The player who was usually the defensive end then moved in to a head-on position with the offensive end. From this position, the player over the offensive end would either play the defense straight, that is, play the offensive end and take care of his responsibility, or he would deal with the fullback who was lined up on the line of scrimmage to his outside. When there was a deal on between the two players, the fullback would smash hard down the line, right off the tail of the offensive end and close the off tackle hole. At the same time, the player over the offensive end would quickly get to the outside to take care of the wide responsibility. On checking the man over the offensive end, it was found that he did not align his feet the same way every time. Upon closer observation, it was noted that when he had his outside foot back, he would deal with the fullback and would take the outside. When his feet were parallel, he would be playing the defense straight, and would not have a deal with the fullback. The tip-off held true regardless of whether the starting end or his substitute was playing. The fullbacks never varied their feet position enough so that any key or tip-off from them was noticeable.

This discovery led to the thought that it might be profitable to check the feet of the rest of the linemen to see whether it could be determined if any of them tipped off the direction he was going to slant or loop. The defensive tackle had a very big stagger in his stance with the right foot back. It was obvious that if he always had his right foot back that far, it would be exceedingly difficult for him to slant or loop to his left. On closer scrutiny, it was seen that if he was going to move to his left on the snap of the ball, he would bring his feet to a near-parallel position.

Army played two basic defensive alignments. One was the Oklahoma 5–4, while the other was a stacked defense similar to a Split 6 alignment. When Army was in the Oklahoma 5–4 alignment, the deep defense would always be a three-deep, but the position of the fullback would vary. At times he would be up on the line of scrimmage to be in position to deal with the end, as previously described, or he would play 3 or 4 yards deep outside of the defensive end. When Army was in a stacked defense, the fullback came up and played on the line of scrimmage as the defensive end. The original defensive end moved in and played head on the offensive end. The defensive tackle on that side moved in and played head on the offensive guard, while the middle guard on the Oklahoma 5–4 took his position head on the other offensive guard. The two linebackers would play directly behind the two men playing over the offensive guards. Regardless of whether Army was in the Oklahoma 5–4 or in the stacked defense, the linebackers did a lot of dealing with the internal linemen.

From the games scouted and several movies that were studied, it was found that it was possible to tell when the end and fullback were going to deal, regardless of the defense. It was also possible to anticipate the move of the defensive left tackle by the position of his feet. In every situation observed, the defensive lineman to the immediate right of the defensive left tackle moved in the direction that the tackle moved, regardless of the defense Army was aligned in. In both defenses, it was fairly evident which holes the linebackers were primarily responsible to cover.

This was information that could be of great value in game preparation, but the question constantly arose as to how much a tip-off of this type could be depended upon for game planning. It was always possible that something like this could be corrected in the two weeks prior to the Navy game. It is not unusual for either team in this classic to make radical changes in either offensive or defensive patterns, although this did not seem likely in Army's case, since Army had been so successful in the games that had been played. Still, it was conceivable that Colonel Blaik might make some changes in his defenses which would neutralize these tip-offs, but it was inconceivable that there would be any noticeable change in the "Lonely End" offense. It just did not seem logical that the offense might be altered, which gave added weight to the possibility that the defenses could be changed.

After long discussion, Navy decided it was inadvisable to base game plans on this tip-off. Theoretically, in order to do so with success, the burden would rest on the quarterback, who would have to check off to a proper play to counteract the deals of the defensive players. With more than 100,000 people in the stands yelling, it would be difficult for him to check off to different plays effectively at the line of scrimmage. The second reason for not basing game plans on the tip-offs was that if Army should correct or neutralize these tip-offs in the ensuing period before the game, Navy would be left in a difficult position. It was decided to let the individual players use the information to the advantage of each concerned. In retrospect, the decision seemed a wise one, although Army did win the game. Unless a person has been directly connected with this great classic, it is difficult to envision the tensions and uncertainties of this game. Under different circumstances, it would be possible to use this type of information to greater advantage. As a matter of fact, this was done during the following football season by another of Army's opponents. One of the assistant coaches of the school involved revealed that the tip-offs had been instrumental in the victory over Army, but the details of how the information was utilized are not known to the author. After the game, the Army coaches were made aware of the tip-offs.

In 1957, Army felt very confident of beating Navy on the basis of two pieces of information which, at first notice, seem inconsequential. From scouting and the study of movies, Army could tell the direction of the slant of the Navy line by the position of the heel of the defensive left tackle. If the tackle's heel was up off the ground, he and the rest of the internal linemen were going to slant to the defense's right. If the heel was down, the slant would be in the opposite direction. This bit of information, plus the position of the quarterback on defense, figured very importantly in Army's game plans. The depth of the quarterback would tell whether Navy was going to be in a two- or three-deep defense. The depth of the Navy quarterback on defense was conveyed with a word signal to the offensive quarterback by the offensive left tackle, who was in a good position to note this. The position of the defensive tackle's heel was conveyed to the Army quarterback by the offensive right tackle with the word signal "up" or "down." If the defensive quarterback was deep, it meant that Navy would be in a three-deep defense, from which Navy had not shown any slanting by the linemen. All of the three-deep defenses that Navy employed that year ended up in a Gap 8 defense on the snap of the ball. This information that Navy was in a three-deep defense gave the Army quarterback the alternative of checking off to a couple of plays that went wide.

If Navy was in a two-deep defense, that meant the line would slant, and the Army quarterback would have an option of checking off to several plays, depending upon the direction of the slant. The burden of determining the defense was divided between the two tackles, and the quarterback then had a possible call to make, depending on whether the play he had called in the huddle would be effective against the defense on that play. The quarterback would have to make the decision as to whether a new play should be called. If he desired to change the play, he would call out a word to designate the new play. Names of colleges were to be the key words. The word Pitt would be the code for one play, while Penn State would mean still another one. The name of any school in Pennsylvania other than Pitt or Penn State would be the check-off for another particular play, while the name of any girl's college would indicate the change to still a different play. A combination of circumstances, and the cheering of some 100,000 fans certainly must have been one of them, was responsible for Army's "busting" signals about five times. Someone on the team would not get the play change, and consequently did the wrong thing. This caused either a mix-up in the backfield action or a missed assignment by at least one of the linemen. These errors undoubtedly caused the players to have a loss of confidence in the check-off system, which might well have affected the outcome of the game. It will never be known what the outcome would have been if these mix-ups had not occurred, and the check-off system thus abandoned.

Unquestionably, one of the big reasons for the success of the 1960 Navy football team was the ability and brilliance of Joe Bellino. This fine athlete was acclaimed the football player of the year and was the recipient of many awards at the conclusion of the season. It would be difficult, if not impossible, to determine his total contribution to his team. Many qualified observers and coaches believed that if a team could succeed in containing Bellino, that Navy would be defeated. This belief was shared by more people after Missouri succeeded in doing just that in the Orange Bowl, and defeated Navy.

Although Joe Bellino had great natural ability, he was also a perfectionist who worked hard to improve himself as a football player. But as gifted and as conscientious as he was, he became the victim of a habit, the knowledge of which could have been used to great advantage by Navy's opponents. Any time that Bellino was going to his right, his right heel was raised to the extent that it was easily detectable. If he was going to move to his left, or pass protect, both heels were flat on the ground. This, too, was clearly visible. Such information could have been valuable to Navy's opponents.

Prior to the ninth game on Navy's schedule, the game against Virginia, this tip-off on Bellino's movement was detected by Navy, but it was not corrected for that game. It was felt that possibly the Army scouts were aware of this tip-off, and it was conceivable that Army could formulate its defensive planning on this piece of information. The variation in Bellino's stance was, however, corrected in the practice sessions prior to the Army game. (It is not known whether this tip-off was ever detected by the Army scouts.)

A variation in a player's stance is more the exception than the rule, but it is more prevalent than many coaches believe. A halfback on Notre Dame's team of 1960 had the same habit that Bellino had, and this information was used by the Navy team. Although this particular player did not see as much action during a game as did Bellino, when he was in the line-up, knowledge of where he was going gave a good indication as to the direction of the play. In the mid-fifties, Duke University had a fullback who changed the position of his feet, depending upon his assignment. When he was going to run up the middle, he would stagger his feet, while he would have his feet in a near-parallel position when he was going off tackle or wide. In the games scouted, every time the fullback staggered his feet, he carried the ball up the middle. When his feet were parallel, usually some play other than the fullback counter was run from the Split T offense.

The positioning of the players' feet is not the only kind of tip-off that the scout should be alert for. Another important area to watch carefully is the varied alignment of the backs.

As confident as Army felt about winning the 1957 game, Navy had its own reasons to be optimistic about the outcome. Navy went into the contest feeling that the alignment of the Army backs would indicate where most of the running plays were going before the play started. Some of the alignments were so pronounced that it was practically certain as to which direction the play was to be run. The linebackers and ends could easily distinguish the backs' varied alignments. Whoever noticed the alignment of the backs would call out a code word that indicated which direction the play would probably go. There was nothing done as far as adjusting any defenses was concerned, the code word simply especially alerted that side of the line which was involved.

Fig. 12–1 shows one alignment of the backs and the plays run from that

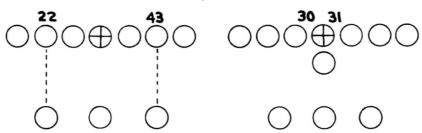

Fig. 12–1. Army's backfield alignment favored for running inside plays.

Fig. 12–2. Army's backfield alignment favored for running the fullback
counter plays.

alignment. Plays 22 and 43 are the straight hand-offs. The backs were
noticeably deeper, and this made running off tackle or wide more difficult,
since the blocking halfback would have a greater distance to go in order to
make his block. It was felt that the probable reason for the depth of the
backs was to give the ball carrier a chance to veer his course if he saw the
opening. This was something that the Army backs had done often and
effectively.

In Fig. 12–2 the backs were noticeably closer to the line of scrimmage,
as well as closer to the fullback. The plays run from this alignment were
the fullback counters from the Split-T series. The diving halfback could
make a quick and effective fake. The other halfback was used to lead the
play, and his close alignment made this maneuver more effective since he
could get to the point of attack quickly.

In the third alignment, as shown in Fig. 12–3, there was a definite
stagger in the alignment, one that was quite evident. The right halfback

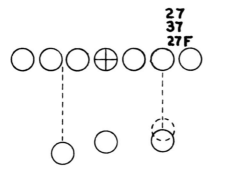

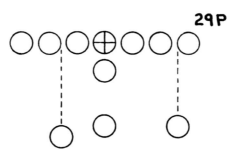

Fig. 12–3. Army's staggered alignment favored for running off tackle to
the right.

Fig. 12–4. Army's staggered alignment favored for sweeps to the right.

aligned himself in an advantageous position to block the defensive end out.
Play 27 was one of Army's basic and most effective plays, as it was the inside
belly play. On this, the right halfback would block the defensive end out,
the fullback would hit over right guard with an excellent fake, and the
quarterback would then hand the ball off to the left halfback as he ran off
tackle. From this alignment of the offensive backs, it would have been
difficult to run any play to the left. Play 27F was another off-tackle play
with the fullback faking over left guard.

In the alignment shown in Fig. 12–4, the right halfback widened his
position in order to have a good angle to block the defensive end in. Several
other plays were run from this setup, but primarily they went wide to that
side, since the right halfback had to make the key block on the end. The
only difference in alignments as shown in Figs. 12–3 and 12–4 was the position of the right halfback. This position was easily distinguished by the defensive end and the linebacker.

Fig. 12–5 shows the alignment from which plays were run to the left side
on sweeps, or the running pass was thrown. The quarterback also gave
the ball to the fullback several times over left guard off the inside belly
series. The left halfback would get in the best position he could to effectively block the end in, and he would change his alignment slightly, but
noticeably, to block the end out, as shown in Fig. 12–6, with either the right
halfback or the fullback carrying the ball off tackle.

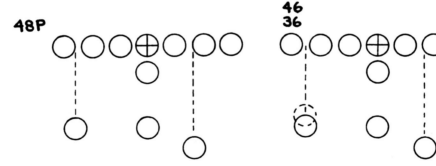

Fig. 12–5. Army's alignment on off-
tackle plays to the left.

Fig. 12–6. Army's alignment on
sweeps to the left.

The different alignments taken by the backs is usually very obvious any
time an offense is run that depends upon the halfbacks to block the defensive ends either in or out. It is something that is easily noticed and can
be used to alert the defensive men to the side on which the offensive men
take an advantageous position to block at the point of attack.

A similar situation occurred during the 1959 and 1960 seasons. One of Navy's opponents, a good football team, would adjust the position and alignment of the backs when the backs went down to their stance from an up position. There were times when this adjustment would not be meaningful, but there were many more times when it was helpful to the defense. In some instances, opponents of this team would have an excellent idea as to where the play was going, while in others they had an excellent idea of where it was not going to be run. For example, if the backs adjusted to an alignment as shown in Fig. 12–3, an off-tackle play could be expected. At other times both halfbacks would move up close to the line of scrimmage as though to get good position to block the end out. In this situation, it was almost certain that no form of wide play was to be run, but a run from tackle to tackle was expected.

The alignment of the ends can also be important, and is another area which should be closely observed by the scout. It is very seldom that a tip-off is uncovered by which you can change your defenses after the offensive team lines up. However, this was possible in a game between Vanderbilt and Miami University, in which Vanderbilt was able to adjust its defenses to compensate for a tip-off.

It was noticed that Miami would have one of the offensive ends take more than a normal split on all plays. There were also times when both ends would split out several yards. After finally ascertaining why they did this, it became evident that the end away from the direction of the play would widen. When both ends would widen, it would be a pass play or a run up the middle. If the play was going to the right of center, and that included going over right guard, the left end would adjust his split. The right end would split on plays to the left. Although it was not known exactly where the play was going, it was known where it was *not* going, and that was to the side of the split end. The threat of a pass was always present, so the defensive backs had to be alert at all times.

The game plans were to go into the game expecting this tip-off to be corrected or neutralized, but if the tip-off did hold up, then the defensive signal caller would call an overshift to the tight end, or a slant or loop away from the split end. The basic defensive alignment was a Wide 6, so this was easily accomplished. The defensive end on the side of the split end would also widen and harass him if he made an effort to get downfield on a pass. The defensive end would then drop off and cover the flat. If both ends split out, the guards were alerted to play for the trap up the middle, while both defensive ends would move out and play head on the offensive ends to keep them from getting downfield quickly for a pass. Vanderbilt was able to blank Miami by a score of 9–0, and the tip-off from the ends was undoubtedly a contributing factor.

There is an interesting sidelight on this game. The following Sunday pictures of the game were shown on television and Don Wade, the captain and defensive signal caller at Vanderbilt, gave the commentary of the game. As Miami would come out of the huddle and line up on offense, he would comment as to the direction the play was going. He called every running play successfully.

A different kind of tip-off was obtained by an alert scout of an opponent of Vanderbilt. At that time Vanderbilt had Bill Wade as its quarterback and passing, naturally enough, was an integral part of the offensive attack. The scout undoubtedly noticed that there were times when the Vandy team got the play quickly in the huddle and got right out to the line of scrimmage, while at other times the team did not get out of the huddle so rapidly. Although it was not obvious to many other scouts, it was evidently detected by this one scout. During the game against this opponent, it was noticed that someone on the visitor's bench would wave a colored handker-chief occasionally, in the manner of giving a signal. It was later established that the scout had timed, and recorded the amount of time, Vandy spent in the huddle before each play. It was evidently found that if the team was in the huddle under a certain number of seconds, the quarterback had called a running play. If the team was in the huddle longer than the figure set by the scout, the play would be a pass. This bit of information proved true often enough that the opponent either was in a defense with maximum coverage, or had a very strong rush on, nearly every time a pass was thrown. This hurt Vanderbilt's strong passing game. This is just another example of a scout's being alert, and when he noticed something different, he was determined to find the answer as to why it was different—in this case, why the team was in the huddle longer at certain times than at others.

Effective scouting, but of a different nature, was evident several times during the 1960 season. One of the most prevalent offensive attacks used in college football has been the Wing T, as developed and popularized by Dave Nelson and Forrest Evashevski. It is generally advocated that the quarterback stagger his feet in lining up to take the snap from the center. Normally, the quarterback will have his right foot back on all plays that go to the right from a Wing Right formation, and will have his left foot back on all plays that go to the left from a Wing Left formation. However, there are usually counter plays in the offense in order to make this key useless, and many teams will have enough counter plays in their offense to throw this key off. There were several major college teams running the offense, how-ever, whose counter plays were limited, especially in the early part of the season, and it was fairly easy to pinpoint the point of attack of the counter plays in their offenses.

For example, if the formation was a Wing Right, and the quarterback had his left foot back, the only plays that were run were those with the left halfback carrying the ball off tackle to the right, the fullback on a trap over the offensive left guard, and the left halfback on a trap over the offensive right guard. If, on the same formation, the quarterback had his right foot back, the only plays back to the left were the wingback off tackle to the left on a counter play where he received the ball directly from the quarterback, or a handoff from the quarterback to the left halfback, who in turn handed the ball to the wingback. One team in particular was stopped cold during the 1960 season because its counter plays were very limited, and the linebackers, in particular, were looking for them. For example, on a Wing Right formation, with the quarterback's right foot back, the linebackers would look to the wingback as soon as the ball was snapped to see if he was coming back on a counter play. If he did not start back as soon as the ball was snapped, the linebackers moved quickly in the direction of the back foot. A bootleg pass or a run by the quarterback off the wingback counter faking undoubtedly would have kept the linebackers honest. However, neither of these plays or any others which would destroy the key were employed in any of the games scouted, so this particular key was played with success.

Another team successfully utilized the key of the quarterback's rear foot, plus keying the linebackers on the offensive guards to lead them to the play. (Keying linebackers on the moves of the offensive guards on an Oklahoma 5–4 defense is very common in defensive football.) From the offensive alignment of Wing Right, with an Oklahoma 5–4 defense, the left linebacker would shoot when the guard in front of him pulled to the left, when the quarterback had his right foot back. The linebacker's course was to go through the gap between the offensive guard and tackle so that the fullback coming up the middle would have difficulty in blocking him. The linebacker was able to penetrate into the backfield and either knock down the pulling end, or tackle the ball carrier before he really got started. The right linebacker would key the same way from a Wing Left formation. When the offensive quarterback had his left foot back on a Wing Right formation, the right linebacker would key on the offensive guard in front of him, and would be ready to shoot when the guard pulled. The linebacker was able to penetrate into the backfield and to stop the plays that were employed by this particular opponent.

In both cases, the opponents playing against the Wing T played defenses based on the offense that had been shown by these teams, and not defenses based on all the possibilities that could be developed from the Wing T formation. The knowledge that the opponent's offense was limited to a certain few plays when the quarterback's feet were aligned a certain way led to the stopping of an offense that might not have otherwise been stopped. Too often the opposing team is given too much credit for being able to do many things offensively that it has not shown. Probably a better approach to game planning would be to play the opponent for what has been shown, but respect that opponent for what it might do. If an opponent gives you something definite to key and play, it seems logical to play the key with some caution, and not gamble that the key is completely foolproof. Play it until the key is proved wrong, or until something more has been added to neutralize the key. But to simply assert that another team *could* do one thing or another does not give that team the ability nor the techniques for such accomplishments. It must be remembered that the opponent's practice time is limited also.

However, it is not the scout's responsibility to decide strategy, although he should be able to recommend or suggest. The scout's prime responsibility is to return from an assignment with as much useful information as possible to satisfy the head coach's demands. The search for tip-offs should be secondary—something that can be pursued as the scout carries out his prime duties. The ability to detect tip-offs can be developed by learning to observe a larger area at one glance, and through a scout's strong desire to improve in all-around ability. Regardless of the level of scouting, the scout should be well prepared for his task, enthused with the challenge that it offers, and aware of the responsibility that scouting carries. Effective football scouting is but one ingredient of successful football, but poor scouting can be primarily responsible for football defeats. It could, undoubtedly, be said that poor scouting has contributed to more defeats than good scouting has accounted for in victories. On this premise, the scout should find it imperative to do his job as effectively as possible, and let the outcome of the game be decided by the other contributing factors and the personnel of the competing teams.

Appendix: Final Report

_____ vs. _____
Team Scouted   Opponent

_____
Date

_____
Site

_____
Weather

_____
Condition of Field

_____
Color of Jersey

_____
Color of Pants

_____
Scout

STATISTICS

_____   _____
Team Scouted   Opponent

Team Scouted		Opponent
_____	First Downs	_____
_____	Yards Rushing	_____
_____	Yards Passing	_____
_____	Passes Attempted	_____
_____	Completed	_____
_____	Intercepted by	_____
_____	Yards Penalized	_____
_____	Punts	_____
_____	Punt Average	_____

157

FOOTBALL SCOUTING REPORT

It is important that you study this form before game time. It is not expected that you will be able to cover all points by seeing one game. The more times you see a team play, the more complete your report should be.

FOOTBALL SCOUTING

1. Do not permit your interest in the game to prevent you from obtaining essential information. Concentrate on one thing at a time.

2. In case of doubt, indicate that information as doubtful or as an opinion.

3. Review any information that has been obtained from newspapers, previous scouting report of this or last season, or pictures. We will have a notebook devoted to a breakdown of various pictures of each team from the previous season.

4. Memorize the numbers of the first two teams.

5. During the pre-game warm up, observe the specialists such as passers, punters, centers passing the ball for punters, kick off men and receivers.

6. Complete the report as soon after the game as is possible while everything is still fresh in your mind.

7. After reading all the newspaper accounts of the game, review your report since some things might be recalled as a result.

8. Hand in only one final report. Gather all the data into one report for presentation.

FOOTBALL SCOUTING REPORT
OFFENSIVE LINE-UP

L. End	L. Tackle	L. Guard	Center	R. Guard	R. Tackle	R. End

Quarterback

Lefthalf	Fullback	Righthalf

List the starting team in the squares and the replacements beneath the squares

OFFENSIVE DISTRIBUTION

Diagram by preference each formation used. Show holes hit by each back and give total times carried through that hole and yards gained. What percent of total offense was each formation used? Use additional sheets as are needed.

TOTAL RUNS AND PASSES IN GAME _____

Total Plays _____   Percentage_____

Total Runs _____   Total Passes_____

Total Plays _____   Percentage_____

Total Runs_____   Total Passes_____

OFFENSIVE
DOWN AND DISTANCE CHART

FIRST DOWN			SECOND DOWN			THIRD DOWN			FOURTH DOWN		
D-D	PLAY	Gn	D-D	PLAY	Gn	D-D	PLAY	Gn	D-D	PLAY	Gn

FIRST DOWN			SECOND DOWN			THIRD DOWN			FOURTH DOWN		
D-D	PLAY	Gn	D-D	PLAY	Gn	D-D	PLAY	Gn	D-D	PLAY	Gn

HOLE SUMMARY

9..............	9..............	9..............	9..............
7..............	7..............	7..............	7..............
3..............	3..............	3..............	3..............
1..............	1..............	1..............	1..............
0..............	0..............	0..............	0..............
2..............	2..............	2..............	2..............
6..............	6..............	6..............	6..............
8..............	8..............	8..............	8..............
Runs Passes	Runs Passes	Runs Passes	Runs Passes

OFFENSIVE PLAY DISTRIBUTION

	PASSES				HOLE DISTRIBUTION							
	Roll Pass	D.B. Pass	Play Pass	Screen Pass	8 Hole	6 Hole	2 Hole	0 Hole	1 Hole	3 Hole	7 Hole	9 Hole
1-Ten												
1-Long												
1-Short												
2-Long												
2-4-5-6												
2-Short												
3-Long												
3-3-4-5												
3-Short												
4-Long												
4-1-2												
INSIDE THE +10 YARD LINE												

OFFENSIVE PLAYS AND BLOCKING SUMMARY

By holes and regardless of formation, show each play run below the line. Above the line, show total times each play was used.

9 Hole   - - - - -   - - - - -   - - - - -   - - - - -   - - - - -

7 Hole   - - - - -   - - - - -   - - - - -   - - - - -   - - - - -

3 Hole   - - - - -   - - - - -   - - - - -   - - - - -   - - - - -

1 Hole   - - - - -   - - - - -   - - - - -   - - - - -   - - - - -

0 Hole   - - - - -   - - - - -   - - - - -   - - - - -   - - - - -

2 Hole   - - - - -   - - - - -   - - - - -   - - - - -   - - - - -

6 Hole   - - - - -   - - - - -   - - - - -   - - - - -   - - - - -

8 Hole   - - - - -   - - - - -   - - - - -   - - - - -   - - - - -

Show the blocking at the point of attack of each play used.

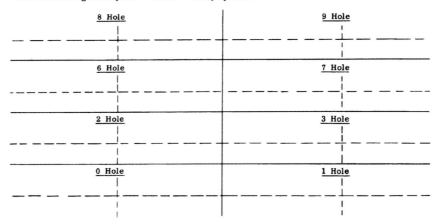

DOWN AND YARDAGE SUMMARY

Does the team have any tendencies such as being "Right-Handed" or favoring the wide side of the field? _____

_____

_____

_____

_____

Does the team pass on a certain down or situation?_____

_____

Give formations, plays and ball carriers favored on short yardage situations_____

_____

_____

_____

_____

Give the same information on long yardage situations_____

_____

_____

_____

_____

Give formations, plays and ball carriers favored inside both 10 yard lines _____

_____

_____

Give scoring plays, formations, ball carriers, and distance _____

_____

_____

Give score, formation, ball carrier and play of two point attempts _____

_____

RUNNING OFFENSE

Diagram and comment on the ''Bread and Butter'' running plays used. Indicate which plays were not seen in any previous games. Use additional sheets to diagram and comment on other running plays used.

RUNNING OFFENSE SUMMARY

What is the strength and weakness of the running attack? _____

_____

_____

_____

_____

Is it primarily an outside or inside running team or does it have a balanced attack? _____

_____

_____

Who is the favorite running back? What are his weapons? _____

_____

_____

Who is the most dangerous running back and what are his weapons? _____

_____

Are there any keys, such as formations or alignments that we can utilize? _____

_____

_____

What is the quarterback's cadence at the line of scrimmage? _____

_____

Is good use made of flankers, or are they decoys? _____

_____

What are the basic line splits and are they varied much? _____

_____

What formations and running plays were used in this game that were not seen in any previous games scouted? _____

_____

PASSING—DOWN - DISTANCE SUMMARY

D-D	Type of Pass	Receiver	Gain	D-D	Type of Pass	Receiver	Gain

FINAL SUMMARY

DOWNS	1st	2nd	3rd	4th
PASSES	. . . . .	. . . . .	. . . . .	. . . . .
RUNS	. . . . .	. . . . .	. . . . .	. . . . .

SUMMARY OF INDIVIDUAL PASS ROUTES

Show the different pass routes taken by each receiver from the alignment shown and indicate the passes thrown to each.

LE
Split

LE
Tight

RE
Tight

RE
Split

LH
"T"

FB

RH
"T"

LH
Flanked
Left

LH
Wing
Left

LH
Wing
Right

LH
Flanked
Right

RH
Flanked
Left

RH
Wing
Left

RH
Wing
Right

RH
Flanked
Right

PASS OFFENSE

By formation, diagram and comment on the pass plays used. Show the down and yardage every time the pass was thrown. Indicate which passes were not seen in any previous game scouted. Use additional sheets as needed.

PASS OFFENSE SUMMARY

What is the strength and weakness of the passing attack? _____

_____

_____

_____

_____

Do the passers indicate quickly to whom they are going to pass? _____

_____

How dangerous as runners are they when rushed? _____

_____

Are there any tip-offs as to screens, such as the passers going deeper to set up? _____

Are screens and draws an integral part of the offense? _____

_____

How effective are the play action passes and when are they used? _____

_____

_____

Does anyone other than the quarterback throw passes? Indicate ability _____

_____

_____

Who are the favorite receivers? Do any have exceptional speed? _____

_____

_____

_____

How effective is the pass protection? _____

_____

_____

DEFENSES

Diagram, explain and give total times each defense was used. Keep all of the same defenses together with the variations and adjustments versus flankers. Discuss any shifting, weaknesses and play of individual players. Indicate which, if any, defenses were not used in previous games. Use additional sheets as are necessary.

DEFENSIVE—DOWN-DISTANCE SUMMARY

List the defenses used as well as the down, distance and position on the field.

First Down			Second Down			Third Down			Fourth Down		
D-D	Defense	Yd. Line	D-D	Defense	Yd. Line	D-D	Defense	Yd. Line	D-D	Defense	Yd. Line

DEFENSIVE ANALYSIS

	DEFENSE	DEFENSE	DEFENSE	DEFENSE	DEFENSE	DEFENSE
1-10						
1-LONG						
1-SHORT						
2-LONG						
2-4-5-6						
2-SHORT						
3-LONG						
3-3-4-5						
3-SHORT						
4-LONG						
4-1-2						

INSIDE THE + 10 YARD LINE

DOWN						
1st						
2nd						
3rd						
4th						

PASS DEFENSE

Discuss the pass defense employed with emphasis on type of coverage, and the ability of the personnel.

TEAM DEFENSES

Diagram and briefly discuss the defenses used by opponents against the team being scouted.

DEFENSIVE SUMMARY

What is the strength and weakness of the running defense? _____

_____

_____

What is the strength and weakness of the pass defense? _____

_____

_____

How well does the team pursue? _____

_____

How far off the ball does the line play and do any of the players slant or loop? _____

_____

Evaluate the guards and discuss their play as to depth, charge and movements _____

_____

_____

Evaluate the tackles and discuss their play as to depth, charge and movements _____

_____

_____

Evaluate the ends and discuss their play as to width and charge _____

_____

Evaluate the linebackers and discuss their play as to depth and movements _____

_____

Do the backs rotate fast to meet running plays? _____

Do they favor rushing the passer or coverage? _____

What linemen get into the pass defense? _____

Is the team vulnerable to screens and draws? _____

What type running and pass plays were successful against this team? _____

_____

PERSONNEL

Give as complete a picture as possible of the abilities of each individual player with emphasis on their outstanding and weak points. (Use a half a sheet or more for each position.)

ENDS

TACKLES

GUARDS

CENTERS

QUARTERBACKS

LEFT HALFBACKS

RIGHT HALFBACKS

FULLBACKS

KICKING GAME—PUNTING

Punters	Steps	Distance	Type of Kick

Diagram the punt formation

How well does the team cover kicks? _____

Can we block any kicks? How? _____

How well do their punters kick when rushed? _____

_____

Has anything else been shown from punt formation other than a kick? _____

_____

Would it be more effective to return rather than try to block a kick? _____

_____

_____

KICKING GAME—PUNT RETURNS AND RUSHES

Diagram the punt returns

How effective has the team been at returning punts? _____

_____

Does it have any exceedingly dangerous returners? _____

Is rushing the punter or returns favored? _____

How effective has the team been at rushing the punter? _____

_____

Are there any tip-offs as to whether the team is going to rush or return? _____

_____

Diagram the punt rushes

KICKING GAME—KICK-OFFS AND KICK-OFF RETURNS

Show the line-up for the kick-off. Circle the safety-man or safety-men.

_____

_____

Kickers	Height	Distance	Direction

_____

_____

How well does the team cover kicks? _____

Where is the team most vulnerable for a return? _____

_____

KICK-OFF RETURN

Who are the most dangerous receivers? _____

What type returns are favored? _____

SUMMARY

What are the strongest phases of the offense? _____

_____

_____

_____

What are the weakest phases of the offense? _____

_____

_____

_____

What are the strongest phases of the defense? _____

_____

_____

_____

What are the weakest phases of the defense? _____

_____

_____

_____

How would you rate the over-all team speed? _____

What is the physical condition of the team in regard to injuries? _____

_____

Is it a well conditioned football team? _____

Is the substitution by teams or individually? _____

_____

How would you rate the over-all depth of this opponent? _____

_____

_____

Index

CPSIA information can be obtained at www.ICGtesting.com

230796LV00002B/86/P